RURAL DEVELOPMENT AND POLITICAL PARTICIPATION AMONG TRIBALS

RURAL DEVELOPMENT AND POLITICAL PARTICIPATION AMONG TRIBALS

By
PRANAB MANGARAJ

ANMOL PUBLICATIONS PVT. LTD
NEW DELHI - 110 002 (INDIA)

ANMOL PUBLICATIONS PVT. LTD.
4374/4B, Ansari Road, Daryaganj
New Delhi - 110 002
Ph.: 3261597, 3278000
Visit us: www.anmolbooks.com

Rural Development and Political Participation Among Tribals

First Edition, 2003

ISBN 81-261-1383-9

PRINTED IN INDIA

Published by J.L. Kumar for Anmol Publications Pvt. Ltd., New Delhi - 110 002 and Printed at Tarun Offset Press, Delhi.

CONTENTS

ACKNOWLEDGEMENTS

This book is substantially based on the findings of my doctoral work. I am indebted to a large number of friends and colleagues who have assisted me in various ways when I was writing the same. The list is a long one and it is not possible to mention each one of them by name. I am particularly grateful to my supervisor Dr. Jayakrishna Baral, Professor of Political Science of Berhampur University, Orissa whose patient guidance has contributed to the quality of the work in no small measure. I express my gratitude to Dr. D. Suren Naidu, Professor of Political Science, Andhra University, Waltair and Professor Dr. Vidya Nand, Professor of Political Science, Magadh University, Bodhgaya who examined the thesis and spared no words to appreciate the work. It was they who insisted that the thesis be published at an early date. I thank them both for their evaluation and kind suggestion.

I sincerely hope and wish that the book proves useful as a work of reference not only to the students and teachers of social sciences but also to the planners and policy makers. Lastly, I hold myself solely responsible for the omissions and the lapses which might be noticed by the discerning reader.

Dr. Pranab Mangaraj

PREFACE

Tribal identity has long since been an issue of much controversy and speculation. The classical colonial ethnographer's depiction of 'tribes' as small, self contained, self-sufficient, homogenous and autonomous communities has been subjected to severe test both by the sociologist and the political economist. The sociologist has tried to describe tribe in terms of the caste orientation as if tribe and caste constitute points in the same social continuum. The political economist, on the other hand, has depicted tribals as members of a peasant class, since 85% of the tribal population are settled agriculturists. In his view, they are the underprivileged sections demanding and justifiably enough, a share in the scheme of secular devolution of power. It is difficult to say which of the two contesting accounts is truer than the other. It is possible that the two depictions are merely hinting at two different phases in the evolution of tribal identity. Tribes acquired the caste dimension first and then moved on to become 'classes'.

However for the sake of analysis the present work assumes that the tribe is a 'class' configuration since a large segment of its population is an integral part of the peasant society and as such, participates in the process of charge. The process of charge has affected the social and economic structure, though in relatively small degrees, by introducing some sort of division of labour. As a corollary of economic differentiation, the traditional economic structure has weakened, no doubt but new political avenues have opened before the tribals. The book makes an attempt to study the pattern of tribal political behavior especially their political participation in the context of changing economic scenario in an in-depth manner. As the study would reveal, tribes have travelled a long distance from the classical ethnographers' descriptions about them.

The developmental experiments have not only resulted in redefining their identity on class lines but also in familiarizing them with the language of modern political discourse. They not only have such prerequisites for political participation as political inclination, a reasonable level of political awareness etc. but they also have political preference, political perception, political perspicacity, and above all a clear prioritisation of needs similar to ours. The level of conscious participation, as the study shows, is striking enough to take a political observer by surprise. The developmental process have endowed the tribals with a bargaining power assisting them to overcome their 'identity' barrier which is epitomized in the ethnological and sociological discussions.

LIST OF TABLES

ABBEREVIATIONS

ABAD: Authority for Backward Area Development
AMCS: Agricultural Marketing Cooperative Societies
ARCS: Assistant Registrar of Cooperative Societies
BDO: Block Development Officer
BEO: Block Extension Officer
CAD: Command Area Development
CCB: Cooperative Central Bank
CD Blocks: Community Development Blocks
CDP: Community Development Programme
CEO: Cooperative Extension Officer
CPA: Community Project Administrator
DCP: District Credit Plan
DDO: District Development Officer
DDP: Desert Development Programme
DPAP: Drought Prone Areas Programme
DPO: District Panchayat Officer
DRDA: District Rural Development Agency
DWACRA: Development of Woman and Children in Rural Areas
EGS: Employment Guarantee Scheme
ERRP: Employment and rehabilitation of the Rural Poor

FFP:	Food for Work Programme
GDP:	Gross Domestic Product
GP:	Gram Panchayat
HYV:	High Yielding Variety
IAAP:	Intensive Area Agriculture Programme
IADP:	Intensive Agricultural Development Programme
IAY:	Indira a Awas Yojana
ICDS:	Integrated Child Development Programme
IRDP:	Integrated Rural Development Programme
ITDA:	Integrated Tribal Development Agency
ITDP:	Integrated Tribal Development Programme
KVIC:	Khadi and Village Industries Commission
KVP:	Kandhamala Vikash Parisad
LAMPCS:	Large Area Multi Purpose Cooperative Societies
LBO:	Lead Bank Officer
MAFCO:	Maharastra Agro Development and Fertiliser Corporation Ltd.
MFAL:	Agency for the Development of Marginal Farmers and Agricultural Labourers
MIDS:	Madras Institute of Development Studies
MLA:	Member of Legislative Assembly
MP:	Member of Parliament
NABARD:	National Agricultural Bank for Reconstruction and Development
NES Block:	National Extension Service Blocks
NGO:	Non. Government Organisation
NREP:	National Rural Employment Programme
NSIC:	National Small and Village Industries Commission
OC:	Other Caste

OSCSTFS:	Oriasa Scheduled Caste and Scheduled Tribe Finance Corporation
PACS:	Phulbani Agency Cooperative Society
PEO:	Fishery Extension Officer
PEO:	Project Evaluation Organisation
PL:	Poverty Line
PLC:	Project Level Committee
PO:	Project Officer
RBI:	Reserve Bank of India
RLEGP:	Rural Labour Employment Generation Programme
RMCS:	Regional Marketing Cooperative Societies
SC:	Scheduled Caste
SEO:	Sericulture Extension Officer
SFDA:	Small Farmers Development Agency
ST:	Scheduled Tribe
TD Blocks:	Tribal Development Blocks
TDCC:	Tribal Development Credit Corporation
TRYSEM:	Training of Rural Youth for Self Employment Scheme
TSP:	Tribal Areas Sub-Plan
UBN:	Unsatisfied Basic Needs
VAW:	Village Agricultural Worker
VLW:	Village Level Worker
WEO:	Welfare Extension Officer

INTRODUCTION

It is an acknowledged fact that precious little has been achieved in the area of tribal development after five decades of national planning. Even concocted figures of statistics have not been able to hide this fact. Various explanations have been offered by social scientists and development experts to this effect, but no one has argued against the path of development *per se*. Furthermore, policy-makers, undaunted by the forebodings of the experts and analysts, have willy-nilly committed themselves to go ahead with the formula exercise partly due to the compulsion of progressive national agenda-setting and partly due to political power-sourcing warranted by electoral mobilisation of tribals.

The Orissan district of Kandhamals (the new name of Phulbani District) presents a unique case for the comprehension of operational dimension of these developmental initiatives. Right form the colonial times, there have been various kinds of interventions in the socio-cultural life of the Kandhas, leading to a process of gradual disintegration of the traditional social relations. In the post-independence period the nature of state intervention has been different from the colonial pattern. It has been a protective as well as welfaristic intervention. Constitutional safeguards have been provided to protect the tribal interest. Reservations of all kinds have been extended to them. Special attention continues to be paid towards the development of tribals in the Five Year Plans. Yet, the process of disintegration continues unabated. What does future hold for them ? This is a challenge before all of us. The present study is an humble attempt to understand the dynamics of social change in the tribal society using two powerful instrumentalities: rural development and political participation.

Organisation of the Study

Chapter 1 seeks to introduce us to the tribals who have been subjected to various interpretations. It also examines the process of their assimilation into the Indian mainstream from the historical standpoint, especially under the British colonialism and after Independence. Introducing the concept of tribal development, it raises some pertinent problems which arise out of the typical cultural milieu of the tribals, the kinship society, the non-monetised character of the economy and the antiquated nature of transactions. It also contains an introductory discussion on the nature of tribal of political participation and its impact on the traditional social hierarchy.

Chapter 2 contains a general profile of the Kandhamala district (the erstwhile Phulbani district) of highland Orissa where the Kandha tribals are mostly concentrated with reference to its history tracing it from the days of dynasty rule through the conquests by Muslims and Marathas to the British rule. It also discusses the manner in which this land of the *Kandhas* came under the British occupation and the heroic struggles of the tribals and the militant Khandayats against the misrule of the Rajas and the Raj to preserve their cultural identity. Since no discussion on the tribe is meaningful without a reference to its culture and cosmology, the chapter focuses our attention on some their religious practices and social rituals like earth worship and the related practice of *meriah,* ancestor worship, practice of sorcery and witch craft etc.. Some aspects of interaction between the tribals and non-tribals especially *Panas* (low caste Hindus) with whom the tribe under study shares a historic relationship have been examined. The district profile contains discussions about geography; climate, rainfall, crops etc., about demography and occupational patterns and about the social infrastructure; education, health, power communication etc.. Furthermore, the chapter seeks to examine the state of poverty prevailing among the tribals and the impact of modernization process on their economy and society.

Chapter 3 deals with concepts and approaches pertaining to development planning, which include growth pole theory and its modified version (growth centre approach). It also discusses the concepts such as sectoral and spatial planning and their relative merits and drawbacks, the concepts of centralised planning and decentralised planning and the concept of multilevel planning. Among the various approaches, the ones discussed in the chapter are the area approach, the target approach, the organisational approach, the marketing approach and the participatory approach, besides the grand approach—integrated development approach. The chapter seeks to study the application of various concepts and approaches in the shape of implementation of various schemes of poverty alleviation and employment generation with particular emphasis on schemes for the development of the tribal population. Lastly, it makes a critical assessment of the performance of the development agencies and the implementation of selected schemes supported through a literature survey.

Chapter 4 focuses our attention on the process of development in the Phulbani district. It studies (i) the schemes under various development programmes and their objectives (ii) the institutional arrangements at the district, the block and the village level (iii) the personnel involved at various stages of implementation of these schemes and (iv) the various sources of institutional finance. It also examines the performances of selected nodal developmental agencies accelerating the pace of development in the district viz. the

Integrated Tribal Development Agency, the District Rural Development Agency etc.. Lastly, there is a critical assessment development programmes and manner in which these have been implemented.

Chapter 5 is rather a micro study involving a discussion of the implementation of development programmes in a gram panchayat, namely Alami with a population size of 2413. Further, it seeks to measure the extent to which these people have been assisted to raise their living standard in the process of development. The chapter contains a detailed profile of all the inhabited villages of the GP. It contains a narrative of the social and economic life of people living in these villages, constructed partly with the help of official data and partly first-hand observation.

In *Chapter 6* we shift our attention from development to political participation. Starling with an analysis of the concept of political participation and the various factors of participation, the chapter makes a study of the nature of political participation among tribals of Phulbani district in the highland Orissa by way of dividing the tribal activities into electoral and non-electoral, and as political and quasi-political. It uses a set of five political variables to measure political participation; these variables are (i) political inclination, (ii) political awareness, (iii) political preference, (iv) political perception and (v) political perspicacity. Further, the chapter seeks to compare the participation of tribals at three levels of politics — national, state and local. Since the main objective of the thesis is to find out the correlation between the process of economic development and political participation, a special effort has been made in the chapter to assess separately the trends of political participation among the tribal beneficiaries and tribal non-beneficiaries and make a comparative analysis of political participation. The sample size used in the case of beneficiaries is 130 (Households) while the one used in case of non-beneficiaries is 65.

***Chapter** 7* seeks the correlate the process of economic development and political participation in the light of the hypotheses and enlists the findings of the study.

1

TRIBAL DEVELOPMENT: ISSUES AND CHALLENGES

TRIBE: PROBLEM OF DEFINITION

A tribe is generally described by anthropologists as a system of social organisation having a common territory, a tradition of common descent, common language, common culture and common name. Some scholars describe tribe as kinship society in which kinship determines all kinds of relationships—social, political as well as economic. C.B. Mamoria[1] describes tribes as 'closed moral communities' and as corporate social organisations. D.N. Majumdar adds the economic dimension when he points out that some Indian tribes are at the food-gathering stage, whereas others are settled agriculturists, just like other non-tribals.

The scheduled tribes in India are also known as adivasis, the original inhabitants — the people who had been long settled in different parts of the country before the Indo Aryans entered and settled down in the Indus Valley. They belonged to different racial stocks, such as Kondid, Gondid, Negrito, Mongoloid, Dravidians etc.. However, there has been no unanimity of opinion in regard to the original race to which the present day tribals belong to.

In India, the term tribe is as much an anthropological category as it is an administrative-legal category. The British census officials used the term to enumerate various 'social' groups in India. The Government of India Act of 1935 used the term 'Backward tribes'. The Indian Constitution of 1950 modified the term slightly using 'scheduled' in stead of 'backward'. By the Constitution (Scheduled Tribes) Order, 1950, issued by the President in exercise of the powers conferred by clause (1) of the Article 342 of the Constitution of India, 212 tribes have been listed as scheduled tribes. Some other groups have been included in the category later on by an Act of Parliament.

Unfortunately, no specific criteria were used by the Government to include or exclude a particular social group from the category of scheduled tribe. Given the problem of definition, political expediency played a key role in determining the list of scheduled tribes. As a result, various state governments gave their versions of what a tribe stand for. Some demographers have criticised the census enumeration of tribals, 'as unreliable and inaccurate'.

With the passage of time, this problem has been pushed to the background in favour of expediency of policymaking for the tribes, in consonance with changes in the larger society of non-tribals. Whether the direction of change in the tribal society is similar to that in the larger society is the subject of our analysis.

HISTORICAL PROCESS OF TRIBAL ABSORPTION

The Incongruent Modes

The expression 'tribal' has often been used to indicate a particular stage of social evolution implying 'certain' distance from the non-tribals in socio-economic terms. However, in India, the tribals and the non-tribal hindus shared religious beliefs and lived harmoniously for hundreds of years. The tribals did not lose their identity and culture in any significant way. In the opinion of Prof. Haimendorf[2] the tribal folks and the Hindu caste society enjoyed a "frictionless coexistence" before the 19th century.

During the 19th century, a lot of changes had come about as a result of the spread of railways and roads. Physical isolation was broken, population growth suddenly increased and land-hungry Hindu peasants, money-lenders and traders penetrated into tribal areas. They not only exploited them but also compelled and coaxed them into abandoning their own cultural traditions and values.

In this context, the views of Prof. N.K. Bose are noteworthy. According to him, the system of property relations prevalent in the non-tribal society determined the nature and mode of tribal assimilation. Prior to the 19th century, the process of assimilation in India took place within the matrix of the Brahmanical social order. But during and after the 19th century, tribals were brought under the colonial administration. Even after India got independence, the colonisation of tribals continued under the façade of democracy. It remains, in essence, exploitative even today.

Historically speaking, the factors mainly responsible for tribal absorption in India are Hinduism and British colonialism. In the preindustrial India, tribals were close to the Hindus in terms of cluture and religion. Other significant elements of continuity between the two are found in economy and social structure. Prof. Ghurye[3] went to the extent of describing tribals (in his reference to the cultural position of aboriginal tribes of central India) as 'Backward Hindus', who must locate themselves in or near the Hindu society. While some of them have been integrated into the Hindu society, bulk of them are closely assimilated. Those living away in the 'recesses of hills and depths of forest' have been marginally influenced by the dominant culture.

The second mode of absorption—a process fostered by British colonialism—was disruptive of tribal solidarity. The collection of revenue, the establishment of the Central Police system and of the judicial system undermined the authority of tribal leaders. This also affected the social solidarity of tribes indirectly.

In course of time, either through cultural closeness with the peasant Hindu society or through the centralised British administration, the tribals at large have been brought to the threshold of transition. Surjit Sinha[4] has observed that the tribal ideology has remained mostly unchanged while their social and economic structures have undergone some transition. There is a noticeable change in the vocational patterns as well as in the mode of exchange of goods and services. In addition, there are "tendencies towards social stratification and feundalization of leadership".

PSYCHO-CULTURAL MILIEU OF TRIBES AND DEVELOPMENT STRATEGIES

It is thus evident that there is a great deal of ambiguity surrounding the definition of tribe. But relative isolation remains a distinct characteristic of tribals even today. Some have viewed this isolation as historical distance from the mainstream, while others especially physical anthropologists have perceived it as genetic distance. However, there is a third view explaining the isolation of tribes in terms of its rigid social structure which is a function of their culture and cosmology. It has been argued that any development strategy meant for the tribals must fuse itself sufficiently with their culture. As B.K. Roy Burman[5] points out, value system trickles in the community response to developmental programmes and specific items of a programme are highly influenced by the corpus of related beliefs and practices.

In areas where there are negative alignment between the two, the strategy of development is bound to be a failure. To cite an interesting example for S.K.Choudhury's study of the *Kandhas* of Orissa (1990)[6], the tribals were supplied milch cattle as part of the government programme. The people got a rich quantity of milk which could not be sold to the fellow tribals primarily because *Kandhas* do not consume milk as part of their cultural tradition. It also could not be exchanged with other groups, because *Kandhas* do not have the knowledge of preservation necessary to enhance its shelf-life and subsequently to transport it for distribution and exchange elsewhere. Choudhury rightly asks the question, should the tribals who do not consume milk be given milk producing cattle? Using a similar instance years ago, Roy Burman[7] attributed the failure of housing programme for the Rabha tribe to this kind negative alignment. The tribals refused to take possession of house because the new settlement was used to house cattle and poultry birds and this, they believed, would invite the wrath of their ancestral spirits.

The administrators are therefore, advised by anthropologists to take cognisance of tribal aspirations and their understanding of and expectations from development programmes[8]. These should be launched on trial basis and on a small scale adapted to their psycho-cultural environment prior to absolute implementation. In the words of Joshi and Srivastava (1989, p. 109) "If changes in material appurtenances and ideological infrastructure are to be successfully initiated, it is imperative that continuity is maintained with the traditional aspects of society."

Apart from those non-economic constraints to development, there are economic constraints as well. Firstly, the shifting cultivation widely practiced in the tribal areas of Orissa even today is uneconomic in character and any improvement in the farming practice is ruled out as long as it exists. Secondly, there is a high degree of indebtedness owing to the absence of durable productive enterprises and extravagant spending on consumption and rituals.

Thirdly there is exploitation by the private money lenders who charge an exorbitant rate of interest 50 per cent or even more. The non-monetised character of the economy aids and abets the exploitation because they cannot get a good price for the forest products that they sell in the markets. They are cheated in weights and measures. Further, they are not actuated by monetary incentives to produce more.

With this backdrop, we would examine the major strategies of tribal development—their nature, foci and implications. One is selective and 'clientele' oriented and the other is interventionist and radical in outlook. Pending this discussion to a later chapter, we take up the problem straightaway.

RESEARCH PROBLEM, OBJECTIVES AND HYPOTHESES

Generally, tribal villages are known for community orientation, close kinship ties and enjoy a fair degree of economic independence from government. In some of them where intensive irrigation is necessary for agriculture, relations between village and government are fairly close. Otherwise, there is a natural distance between government and village which is characterised by strong parochial ties of kinship. The tribal has little to do with rule of law as he would support his kinsmen in any dispute and expect others to do so.

The kinship factor also prevents the growth of political parties with a broad membership. In the event of his recruitment to a political party, a tribal would use the party to channelise his grievances and needs which are strictly local in character.

The static class structure of the village stands on the way of political development. Thus peasant is strictly differentiated from the official and the clerk. He is closer to, though still distinct from, the small trader and artisan. Class relationships are precisely defined in the traditional mould, linguistic and sartorial distinctions being usual. There was no class conflict in these societies. Economic and social development tend to throw up new classes which are difficult to accommodate within the traditional class structure. The class conflict that ensues as a result of this disturbs the social equilibrium. The social tension resulting from development interventions manifests in electoral and extra-electoral mobilisations.

The tribal society can be viewed as a 'consummatory system' the stability of which depend on the beliefs and attitudes prevailing in that society. In this type of society, innovation is seen as alien to the values permeating the social and political system. In this consummatory society, the state, the authority and the like are all parts of an elaborately sustained high-solidarity structure in which religion is pervasive as a cognitive guide. Apter[9] uses the contrasting experiences of political development of two African States, Uganda and Ghana, which he describes as instrumental and consummatory systems respectively. While instrumental Uganda witnessed political development in the sense of greater centralisation of state power, consummatory Ghana moved faster with regard to political participation. The latter's experience in participation was the outcome of breakdown of traditional framework of belief through westernisation and the strife between different centres of power.

Huntington's[10] thesis is that modernisation produces instability. Twisting it slightly, we may say economic development causes social mobilisation. People are 'disrupted socially form the traditional pattern of life, confronted with pressures to change their ways, economically, socially and politically, bombarded with new and "better" ways of producing economic goods and services and frustrated by the modernization process of change generally and the failure of their government to satisfy their ever rising expectations. When economic growth is rapid, the effects are still more devastating. It produces *nouveau riches* who are imperfectly adjusted to and assimilated by the existing order and who want political power and social status commensurate with their new economic position. It also aggravated regional and ethnic conflicts over distribution, investment and consumption and increases capacities for group organisation and consequently the strength of group demands on government which the government is unable to satisfy.[11]

Increase in literacy, education and exposure to mass media as a result of economic growth raises people's aspirations to a level of buoyancy which, instead of tranquilizing the population, promotes a spirit of unrest. Political participation by literates with aspirations is bound to pose threat to the system as a whole. However, if there are opportunities for social and economic mobility and adaptable political institutions, there would be less of instability.

Political participation gets expanded as demands on government grow. In the absence of political institutions, demands cannot be expressed through legitimate channels and aggregated within the political system. A sharp increase in political participation is likely to produce instability in terms of demand for demands enforcement.

Extrapolating from the above analysis we may say that economic development, in the sense of meaningful contribution to the living standards of people, raises their aspiration level. It breaks their cognitive barriers of culture and produces participation, both social and electoral. On the other hand, economic deprivation produces apathy, because people are too poor to protest and assert their rights.

Both the processes give rise to activities indicating change in the social and political system. Political participation which accompanies such process may vary in nature and degree depending the inputs and their combination pattern in a particular social context.

The broad objectives of the present study can be stated of follows:

It seeks to examine the assumption that the developmental benefits lead to a rise in standard of living of tribals and the other poor. It also intends to find out if there is a corresponding change in the political life of beneficiaries. The widely accepted interface between the economic man and political man will be critically evaluated.

The standard of living of the people has been assessed with reference to their occupational mobility, *per capita* family income, consumption pattern and their access to basic civic amenities such as education and health. The quality of political life has been assesed by examining different kinds of electoral activities like voting, campaigning, contesting elections, agitations etc. and evaluating cognitive political behaviour as reflected in political interest, political awareness, party affiliation, political perspicacity, and political efficacy.

The following hypotheses have been tested in the present study.

1. The developmental benefits contribute to rise in the standard of living of the people.
2. The implementation of developmental programmes encourages occupational diversification and occupational mobility.
3. Developmental programmes contribute to increase in the awareness and activism of the beneficiaries.
4. Economic development stimulates social and political participation.
5. Political participation at the grass-roots level brings about a change in the traditional power structure.
6. Political participation prepares a favourable social climate for modernization of tribals.

7. Political participation produces capacities for group organisation and thus, social groups; vying for power and identity.
8. Political participation increases bargaining power of tribals vis-a-vis other social groups and vis-a-vis the state.
9. Political participation brings about a change in the elite profile.
10. Deprivation from development benefits, in stead of leading to indifference and non-participation, often leads to political mobilisation in the form of protest.

METHODOLOGY

The method adopted for the testing of the hypotheses outlines above is partly qualitative and partly quantitative. The qualitative part consists of on-the-field investigation and participant observation. The quantitative part consists of data collected by the use of questionnaire accompanied by interviews. Interviewing the respondents while filling-up the questions was necessary because the respondents while filling up the questions was necessary because the respondent's grasp of questions was very poor. Often, assistance of the relatively more educated villagers was sought for the purpose.

Field data have been collected only after visiting 3 to 4 villages lying in different clusters as a part of the rapport building exercise, and as a preliminary step to study the viability and relevance of the project.

DATA COLLECTION

Data collection in the field was done in three different phases, between 1994 summer and 1995 autumn. A total of ninety days have been spent in the field covering 14 villages.

Data used have been categorised into general, economic and political. General Data covers information about beneficiary category, social affiliation, sex, occupational status and education. Data relating to per capita household income, per capita household expenditure, and institutional finance come under the economic category. Political data include election data for the Gram Panchayat, the Assembly constituency and the Parliament constituency. These data cover issues regarding various activities directly or distantly related to political participation.

While collecting field data, care has been taken to distribute the work into two parts: Collection of general and economic data preceding that of the political. This has been done in order to separate the two kinds of activities for the sake of analysis. Thereafter, the interplay between the economic structure and the political process is examined. To facilitate this, the questionnaire was split into two sets and administered in succession rather than at one go.

The socio-economic profile of the newly created GP has been labourously constructed since no readymade literature is available. The village agricultural worker, the agricultural overseer, agricultural extension officer and the village level worker working for the GP were particularly helpful. My own students of the Government College, Phulbani, hailing from the villages being studied, have co-operated in the construction of the data base for the Gram Panchayat.

It is useful to point out here that my long stint as Lecturer in the P.G. Department of Political Science for more than six years from August 87 to Dec. 1993 stood me in good stead. It gave me the rare opportunity to acquaint myself with the place, the people and the conditions of their living. Besides, I received help from some school teachers, officials in the district headquarters, bank officials, journalist-friends, and some senior citizens of the Phulbani town. I have tried to blend my own first hand intimate knowledge with the outside sources of information rather objectively.

NATURE OF OFFICIAL DATA AND THEIR LIMITATIONS

I would like to place on record some lapses and limitations of the present study. The official sources like District Statistical Office, District Planning Office have not yet come up with any concrete data base for the new G.P. the stray informations available have not yet been brought up to date. The Village Index Card System which has been introduced is far from comprehensive. However, the District Informatics Centre is currently busy compiling village data under the supervision of District Planning Unit. It is hoped that this would help the researcher in building up the base of his research as well as save his precious time, energy and money.

Here, we would like to say that the data available at the offices in the Block, Tehsil and District are not always reliable. Sometimes the statistical data are manufactured by the statistical investigators, while in case of those relating to income, land holding size of tribals etc., official figures are anything but authentic. Using such data alone will surely impair the research in a big way. Further, data already available are not revised and updated so as to take stock of the changes which have occurred over time. To the extent possible, I have tried to incorporate the latest data available in the field at the time of fieldwork. The data on income of beneficiaries collected from the Block Office, were found unreliable. Therefore, I had to depend on data collected form the field exclusively. In stead of accurate figures of income, I have used income grades to determine the economic status of the beneficiary. By income, I mean the *per capita* family income from all sources.

SECONDARY DATA SOURCES

The secondary data have been collected prior to the field investigation, and from a number of official and semi-official sources. Among the sources tapped at Phulbani, mention may be made of the District Rural Development Agency, Integrated Tribal Development Agency, Block Office, Tehsil Office, District Collectorate Library, District Statistical Office, District Panchayat Office, District Election Office etc. Besides, I have relied on some libraries, institutes, offices, departments located at Bhubaneswar. Some of them are mentioned here. They are: The Tribal and Harijan Research Training Institute, Department of Harijan and Tribal Welfare, Department of Panchayati Raj, Department of Rural Development, Bureau of Economics and Statistics, Legislative Assembly Library, Secretariat Library etc. Materials have been collected from Nehru Memorial Museum Library and JNU Library located at Delhi.

THE SAMPLE AND THE QUESTIONNAIRE

The questionnaire was administered to a sample of 130 beneficiary households selected at random and evenly distributed among all the villages of the G.P . The sample size is both large and exhaustive and investigation, intensive and comprehensive. Out of a total of 604 households coming under the G.P, a sample covering more than a quarter of the total has been taken. The details of beneficiaries such as their family size, land size, occupational status, sex, education etc. have been collected from District Rural Development Agency and updated, wherever necessary, at the Block Office with the help of the Progress Assistant in charge of programme implementation and the village level worker attached to the GP. The list thus collected has been used to ensure that no wrong information is furnished by the respondent. At the same time, we have been able to detect wrong and obsolete official data in the course of our field investigations.

SOME ASSUMPTIONS

We have assumed that the economic wellbeing of people in a backward tribal society is largely the outcome of the government's development initiatives and that it produces greater political participation among people during the elections and otherwise.

We also assume that the correlates of political participation per se are as significant as voting and other allied electoral activities The former constitute the *raison d'etre* of political life of the people. Among them, general interest in village affairs, party affiliation, political preference, political awareness, political efficacy and political perspicacity are worth-noting.

The GP under study has a mixed population comprising *Kandhas. Panas* and other non-scheduled lower castes. We have tried to divide the beneficiaries into economic groups on the basis of criterion adopted in the Integrated Rural Development Programme. Those people within the income less than Rs. 11,000 have been treated as below the poverty line. On the basis of income-grades, we have devised five categories, each within a margin of Rs. 4,000 from the other with the exception of the last one. The first three categories come under the poverty line while fourth and fifth categories are treated as having moderate and high standard of living respectively. The underlying assumption here is that the general response regarding their standard of living is determined by the income level.

While economic status is an important factor, it is not the only factor of political participation. Nor is it always its most important factor. It is assumed that education may significantly contribute to the political awareness and political participation of an individual. We have therefore, divided our respondents into five categories with illiterates at one end and highly educated at the other.

Another factor indirectly influencing political participation is the gradual occupational diversification taking place even in a closed system like the tribal village. Instead of being totally confined to traditional occupations, the tribals have tended to shift away to new ones. This occupational shift has resulted in the growth of a number of mixed occupational groups with corresponding change in their economic status. In the changing economic scene of the tribal society, occupational diversification and shift, mixed occupational groups and status change are important phenomena.

Political participation at the local, state and national levels has been examined to show the relative quality and effectiveness at three levels. The degree of political awareness is examined at three respective levels. Grievance redressal is another means employed to know if justice is dispensed locally or by depending on the administrative and judicial machinery accessible to them.

In brief, the present study undertakes to analyse and assess the interface between the economic man and the political man.

REFERENCES

1. C.B. Mamoria, *Tribal Demography of India* (Allahabad, Kitab Mahal, 1957).
2. Christopher Von Furer, Haimendorf, "Tribal Problem of India," "*A Discourse at The National Institute of Rural Development* (Hyderabad) Dec. 18-27, 1985.
3. G.S. Ghurey, *The Aboriginals So-called and their future*, (Pune, Gokhle Institute, 1943)
4. Surjit Sinha, "Tribe-Caste and Tribe-Peasent Continua in Central India", *Man in India* (New Delhi) 45, 1, 1965.
5. B.K. Roy Burman, *Towards Poverty Alleviation Programmes in Nagaland and Manipur* (Delhi, Mittal Publications, 1984).
6. S.K. Choudhury , "Tribal Development: Dimensions of Planning and Implementation", *Indian Anthropologist* (New Delhi) June–December 1990, pp. 49-66.
7. B.K. Roy Burman, *Towards Poverty Alleviation Programmes in Nagaland and Manipur* (Delhi, Mittal Publications, 1984).

8. Nita Mathur, "Evolving Strategies for Tribal Development", Strategies for Tribal Development, *Mainstream* (New Delhi) 7 March 1992, pp. 17-22.

9. David E. Apter, *Political Change* (London, Frank Cass, 1973).

10. Samuel P. Huntington, *Political Order* in *Changing Societies* (Princeton, Yale University Press, 1968).

2
THE STUDY AREA

HISTORY OF BOUDH-KANDHAMALS

The early history of Boudh-Kandhamals is obscure and far too difficult to comprehend. Attempts, however, have been made to reconstruct it form the stray anecdotal accounts of the early rule of dynasties of the region. Pandit Binayak Mishra's account has reference to 'Khinjali Mandala' which consisted of Boudh and Ghumusur. One Silabhanja was its first ruler. The Bhanjas were a line of vassal kings to Bhaumakaras whose power extended from the Ganges in the north to the Mahendragiri in the South. For a long time, the Bhanja dynasty ruled Boudh and Ghumusur until it was threatened by Sulkis and Somavamsis.

With the death of Nettabhanja II, Boudh was separated from Ghumusur and each of them was ruled by a separate line of the Bhanja clan. The Sulkis invaded the Angul region of the Bhanja territory and pushed the Bhanjas towards Boudh. The Somavamsi king Janmejeya I Mahashivagupta of Kosala (Sambalpur-Bolangir) in his drive for territorial expansion fought and killed Ranabhanja who ruled Boudh for sixty years. Boudh-Kandhamals came under the Somavamsis who united Utkal with Kosala.

The Somavamsis could not keep such a vast territory under them for long and the powerful Cholas took over under the leadership of Rajendra Chola. Although the Bhanja dynastic rule had come to an end, some Bhanja rulers survived to serve as tributary chiefs, the notable ones being Solan Bhanja and Kanaka Bhanja, lending support to the Cholas in times of need.

The Chola rule came to an end with the Kalachuris defeating the last Chola king Someswar III in about 1119 A.D. Once again, there was instability when the Kalachuries were challenged and defeated by the Gangas in 1220 A.D. Boudh along with Sambalpur and Sonepur came under the Ganga rule. The legend has it that between the decline of Somavamsis and the rise of the Gangas, there was a Brahmin dynastic rule under Gandhamardhan Dev. The successor to him was his adopted son from Bhanja line, named Ananga Bhanja who came to be known as king Ananga Deb. This inaugurated a new line of kings and plan of territorial expansion.

The territory of Boudh remained the main area of contact for the muslims, the Marathas and the Britishers, in successive order. The muslim contact was rather insignificant. The Marathas were successful in imposing a revenue administration on the territory during their rule. The Britishers terminated the Maratha rule over Boudh in 1826 when Boudh alongwith Athamalik was ceded to the British by Madhoji Bhonsle Appa Sahib. Boudh remined part of the South-West Frontier Agency under one Governor-General for about 10 years. It was brought under the Superintendent of Tributary Mahals, Cuttack in 1837. The territory of Boudh under the Boudh Raj family had in the course of time been subjected to a process of dismemberment in the form of separation of Daspalla, loss of Panchar Pargana, separation of Athamalik and Kandhamals.

The account of separtion of Kandhamals from Boudh is very fascinating. L.S.S.O malley had pointed out that the

Raja of Boudh had no effective control over Kandhamals in practice, in spite of his overlordship over that tract of land. In 1837, Mr. Ricketts had reported that he had no power over his Kandha subjects in 1844 Mr. Mills stated that *Kandhas* had long been at feud with him, paid no revenue, were under no kind of control and were in the habit of making encroachments on the lands of the Raja. Madhav Konhar and Nabaghana Konhar were two influential chieftains, who defied Raja's authority.

Added to this defiance, the Ghumusur Rebellion of 1853-54 following the passing of the Act for the suppression of Mariah sacrifies of 1848 in the Orissan hill tracts led to the British conquest of Kandhamals and its subsequent annexation. Under the *Meriah* Suppression Act, Boudh, Daspalla and some other regions were brought under the direct charge of the Agency appointed by the Governor-General in Council for the suppression of human sacrifices prevailing at that time.

In protest against the British supression, Dora Bisoi and his nephew Chakara Bisoi took shelter in Bissoipada (now Bisipada) and continued their guerilla warfare against the British. From there, Chakara Bisoi carried on his armed depredations in adjoining Ghumusur and in parts of Dasapalla and Nayagarh. He succeeded, time and again, in evading the pursuit of agency troops and those of the Boudh chief.

About the year 1855, Boudh state was put under the Superintendent of Tributary Mahals of Orissa, Mr. Samuells. A stockade police thana was set up and one Agent or Tahasildar was appointed to bring the Mahals under control. This marked the formal annexation of Kandhamals by the Britishers.

The Prominent Rajas of Boudh during the British Rule were Sri Chandrasekhar Deb, Shri Pitambar Deb, Sri Jogendra Deb and Shri Narayan Deb. Some of them were granted Sanads in recognition of their loyalty to the British

Government and their role in the suppression of human sacrifice as well as in the Ghumusur rebellion.

Raja Pitambar Deb and Raja Jogendra Deb received Sanads in 1875 and 1894 respectively. During the reign of Narayan Deb, a political agitation was organised by the secret association in 1930–32 which was mercilessly put down.

Since the suppression of Kandha uprising up to the year 1930, there was practically no mass agitation in the ex-state of Boudh. In 1938, there were widespread agitations in the feudatory states of Orissa, especially against the Rajas of Nilgiri, Dhenkanal, Talcher, Ranpur etc. In 1945 the Prajamandal under the leadership of late Damodar Dandasi launched a popular movement in Boudh against the misrule of the Raja and state officials and demanded constitutional reforms. It was later suppressed by the Raja with the help of the State police. However, there were sporadic agitations against forest laws, free labour extracted for catching elephants. Besides, there were student agitations. But all these made little difference to the political condition of the people.

CULTURE

Having examined the chronology of events that led to the creation of Kandhamals, it would be proper to look into the ways of life, the belief systems, rituals and religious practices of the *Kandhas,* because these give them an identity as a community as well as spiritual sustenance. The totality of their experience, both psychic and spiritual, and the spatial context of the tribals need to be looked into for a proper analysis of their development.

In the Kandha society, man, nature and supernatural are all bound within a common boundary of relationships. In the man-nature relationship, the beliefs show the natural universe to be continuous with the human world of interactions and sentiments. To the Kanadhas, earth is not something to be used, not a possession nor an object of exploitation, but a living entity and an object of worship. It is both sacred and intimate. The rituals of the terra matter refer man back to his primaeval association with the earth and the symbolic assumption of organic link with mother Earth.

There is a myth in the Kandha society that the Earth deity was the first Kandha woman who came out of the earth and at her own request became the first human sacrifice. This act of hers imposed an obligation on the *Kandhas* to make regular offerings of blood to propitiate her. In exchange, she would grant fertility and wellbeing. The earth, thus, became the spiritual ancestor through whom lineal descent, as the belief goes, could be traced. All of them are born of her, "in the same way", to quote Mircea Eliade, "the Earth with her inexhaustible fecundity gives birth to the rocks, rivers, trees and flowers". Cultivating earth was fraught with guilt and fear. It was seen to be an act of pollution or defilement. Rites are performed and a meriah is sacrificed to propitiate her. Fertility of land depended on whether the deity had been appeased. Drought and famine were attributed to neglect in making the necessary offerings to the deity.

Meriah (now done with buffalo substitutes) is a complicated ritual performed in stages with a gap of every three to five years. The invocatory song accompanying the sacrifice is sung in three parts. In the first part, the villagers go to the house of village headman on the day of sacrifice and symbolically purchase the object, the buffalo which is like his child. The second song is sung by the priest (Jani) as he inflicts the first stab on the buffalo with his pick-axe. The third is a chorus sung by all villagers, invoking Dhartani, the earth mother, to bestow prosperity and plenty on the entire village community. Representatives from neighbouring villages, attend the ritual and receive the required slice of flesh and blood to take back and bury it with a morcel at the Darni stone in their fields, in a symbolic gesture.

The *Kandhas* are greatly indebted to their ancestors for their spiritual sustenance in their day-to-day life. They believe that, the living and the dead form a mutually dependent community, each present to the other and each equally belonging to the kin-group into which they were born. The departed are especially concerned in the birth, marriages and deaths of their living kin. They cultivated the same hill-plots and fields which are now held in trust by the living to be passed on in good condition to the unborn. In recognising their ancestors, the *Kandhas* reaffirm the relationship of the present generation with its immediate and distant past, and their responsibility for maintaining harmony within the whole of the community.

The *Kandhas* believe strongly in sorcery and witchcraft as effective forms of retribution. These are practiced by the ill-wishers and evil-doers for their selfish gain. Sorcery follows the classic method of obtaining shed hair, nail pairings, soil from victim's footprint or sputum, or some closely personal possession, for that retains owner's life force and can be used to have spoken a curse over them, the effect on the victim can be powerful and rapid. Evil eye is more common form of ill-wishing. It becomes effective simply through a direct glance without the knowledge of the victim. A curse may simultaneously be spoken or simply articulated in the mind.

Witchcraft is the most feared form of evil doing. The witches work at night by stealing the soul of their sleepy victims. The practitioner chews up a man or a woman right inside, so that the person later falls ill and dies. The soul is then kept in captivity by the witch until body wastes away, having lost the life force at its centre. When the victim believes that his/her life soul has been taken, result is too often steady decline to death. Following such death, the corpse is cremated in normal way because the part of one's soul which becomes an ancestor (in this process) is industructible even by witchcraft. *Kandhas* also believe in evil-doers' power of transforming themselves into tigers or snakes with the intention of causing harm to others. Some believe that the transformed tiger or leopard becomes a man-eater.

Good or bad, these beliefs in the presence of ancestors, spirits and deities provide the community with a basic sense of identity and are marked by great spontaneity. There is little desire to achieve high status and the aspirational level in terms of material achievement is low.

In short, a deep attachment to and intimate love of this world, the ancestral village, and life, here and now, are what the Kandha culture stands for. Sarabu, the character in the celebrated fiction of Gopinath Mohanty "Amrutara Santana' typifies amply the world view of these people who have been described as the 'primitives' and the indigenous people, the pre-literate or the scheduled tribe. The process of economic growth and development has led to gradual marginalisation. To quote S.K. Mohapatra, "They *(Kandhas)* have, over periods of documented and known history, moved or been pushed away from the plains and fertile lands to hills and jungles; elsewhere even to reserve forests and earmarked habitations".

TRIBE-NON-TRIBE INTERACTION

The tribals are poor, disadvantaged and educationally backward. A close look at the government's tribal policy would reveal that adaptation of tribals has taken place, to a great extent, at the expense of themselves. Their interaction with non-tribes has resulted, in course of time, in mutual socio-economic dependence between the two. Studies have shown how non-tribes have influenced the tribes leading to socio-cultural changes. Dutta Majumdar draws our attention to the influence of Hinduism on Santal culture. According to him, the impact of Hindu landlords, money-lenders and traders on the economic life of Santals has been more conscious." (1956, 53-54). In north-east India, interaction between tribes and non-tribes in the political arena has been of a competitive nature. 'The tribes had been and continue to be in conflict with non-tribes, leading in some instances to serious hostilities. The hostilities have led even to armed confrontation'. However, the frame of reference of tribes for social interaction is rapidly undergoing a change with the expansion of communication, intensification of contact and gradual induction into the technological order.

Fear of loss of identity is the probable cause of low level of interaction with non-tribe. Acculturation is a process of subsequent change in the original culture patterns of other tribes or both tribes and non-tribes. The process of assimilation is viewed as loss of identification and cultural identity on the part of numerically smaller tribes who become a part of the non-tribe Indian civilization. Integration has been viewed as a continuous process of mutual give and take between tribes and non-tribes. It essentially denotes an historical acceptance of the cultural differences and tolerance of each other. In the process of integration, tribes have not lost their identity and continue to maintain many of their cultural traditions.

After independence, the rate of interaction has accelerated in all parts of India *with,* increasing socio-economic dependence between the two. To be more precise, it has meant acculturation of tribes, in the area of material culture, tribals taking to the use of goods manufactured by outside groups. The reverse is also true, though not to the same extent. The tribal way of life is affected in the process but not lost, in toto.

In Kandhamals, this interaction may be seen as forced and as an outcome of a policy of usurpation and expropriation by the government in the matters of land and forest. Land is most precious to the *Kandhas,* since it links them to their past and future and gives them their identity. They see themselves as true owners of land, hills and forests. Their feasts festivals, marriages and general mobility have their roots in land. Secret sale of land is not allowed, for transactions are between family groups, and not between individuals.

During the past thirty years, the transfer of land to the non-tribals (Oriyas) has been enormous. Furthermore a few affluent Kandha land-owners started to take land on lease from the poorer and the needy *Kandhas.* The influence of outsiders has brought about a change of attitude between rich and poor *Kandhas* based only on economic differentials. Democratic power structures have come whetting up the appetite for individual gain.

The Orissa Areas Transfer of Immovable Property (by STs) Regulation 1956 was intended to protect the tribal people in matters of ownership of land. However, it made a concession in that it allowed the sale of land to non-tribals with the permission of the Project Director, ITDA. Permission has been granted liberally leading to large scale land transfers to non-tribals in ITDA areas of Kandhamal district.

The indebtedness leading to land mortages has also led to practical alienation of large tracts of tribal lands facilitated through the law of Adverse Possession of 12 years. *Podu* cultivation is carried on at the higher and lower hill slopes by the tribals without any Rayati Rights. This makes *podu* fields alienation-prone. The tribals find it very difficult to legally defend ownership of their lands and settle possession disputes because of their poverty and total ignorance of the revenue and forest acts.

Forest is a great asset of the tribals. It is a provider of means of livelihood, materials of house construction, herbal remedies and raw materials for household and cottage industries. It is also the focus of social and religious life. A sense of personal relationship with forests permeates Kandha life. Britishers systematically expropriated the tribal ownership by passing forest Acts in 1865 and later, in 1878 with amendments. Forests became a source of revenue to the government. Tribals migrated from forest in search of alternative means of livelihood. The outsiders took advantage of state policy to deplete the forest for trade purpose.

The Dhebar Commission Report of 1961–62 called for a basic change in forest policy. It recommended the return of this resource base to the tribals and restore the balance in their economy. However, the National Commission on Agriculture, being keen on the 'rational use of forest' emphasised its potential for providing employment to the local people and ignored their rights on it.

Reserved forest areas progressively alienated the tribes from forest. They were denied rights over the timber and the minor forest produce such as Kendu leaves, Sal seeds, Mahula flowers etc. The price mechanism operated by the government put them at a perpetually losing position. The TDCC, LAMPCS entrusted with the marketing of forest produce were responsible for further marginalisation of tribals.

General Profile of Kandhamal District

The undivided district of Phulbani was formed way back on 1 January 1940. It had until 1994, two distinct geographical regions, namely, the river plains of Boudh Sub-Division and the hilly-cum-forest tracts of Phulbani and Baliguda Sub-Divisions. This variation in physiography of the two regions had a corresponding variation in their climatic conditions as well as in the way of life of the people.

Kandhamal district was formed during the Janata Rule in 1994 following an unprecedented tribal agitation for a new identity and status for the *Kandhas*. Boudh Sub-Division was separated from Phulbani District and accorded the status

PLATE 1

MAP OF THE PHULBANI DISTRICT

SCALE = 1" = 10 MILES

YEAR - 1994

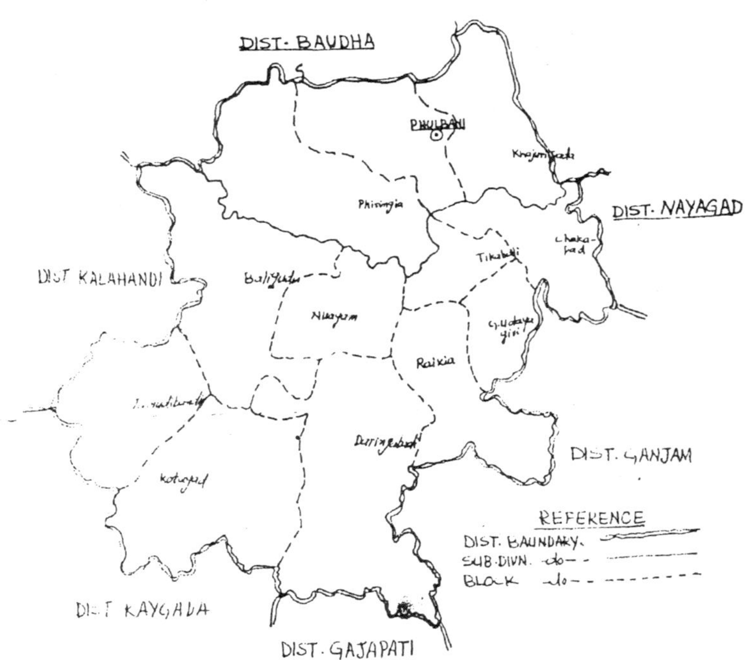

of a district. The new Kandhamals district is mainly a plateau with an altitude varying between 1600' to 3000'. The climate is sub-tropical hot and dry summer, cold and humid monsoon and cold and dry winter. The rainfall is erratic with uneven distribution, often resulting in drought conditions. In 1994 the actual rainfall recorded was 2093 mm though the normal rainfall in 1580 mm. The new district spreads over a territory of 7649.2 *km* with a density of 71 per *sq. km.* The sex ratio is almost even. The scheduled caste and scheduled tribe population account for 51.51 per cent of the total population. With a predominant tribal population, scheduled caste and scheduled tribe population stand at a ratio of 1:2. The rural population has shown a steady increase by a margin of 20.51 per cent in ten years time (1991 Census Data), closely following the overall population growth rate which is 21.69 per cent. Out of a total population of 546281 in the entire district, a huge majority 510619 live in rural areas of the district (1991 Census). Kandhamal district has now three Sub-Divisions, namely, Phulbani, Balliguda and G.Udayagiri. There are of 4 Tahasils, Blocks, 144 Gram Panchayats and 2515 villages under its administrative jurisdiction.

The district has the distinction of being the most backward district in Orissa in respect of industrial development. Cultivation and collection of forest produce continue to be the main occupation of large majority of people. The state of agrarian economy remains extremely poor. The hilly-terrain, scarcity of water-supply and power shortage have stood in the way of growth in a big way. The percentage of cultivable area in relation to the geographical area is 39.1 per cent which is the lowest in the state. While per capita availability of cultivable area at 0.53 hectare is highest in the state, the per hectare consumption of fertiliser at 5.4 kg is lowest in the state. The yield rate of food grains at 9.91 qntls per hectare is the second lowest in the state[1].

The major crops sown and produced are rice, maize, mung, biri, kulthi, til, mustard and groundnut. The total irrigated area through minor flow and lift irrigation projects is 16.78 hectares. The district has a large forest area covering 4729 *sq. km* which is 61.82 per cent of the total geographical area (1993 Statistics). Fish production (pisciculture) has been good in recent years; in 1993 the district had a fish production of nearly 479 metric tonnes.

THE SOCIAL INFRASTRUCTURE

The overall social profile of the Kandhaml district speak of its dismal state of development.

EDUCATION

The district has a poor showing compared to other districts of the state as far as educational attainments are concerned. There are 234 primary schools, 36 middle schools and 13 secondary schools per one lakh population. The teacher-pupil ratio at three levels is 1:4, 1:18 and 1:10 respectively. In contrast, the schools started by Harijan and Tribal Welfare Department reveal a better picture in respect of teacher-pupil ratio at the primary and middle school level that is, 1:23 and 1:16 respectively. While the teacher-pupil ratio of 1:19 in these schools at the secondary level is worse than the general schools. The total number of schools (of both categories) in the district are given in the following table:

Table 2.1
Schooling Facilities Available in the District

Level	*General Category*	*Ashram Category*	*Total*
Primary	1279	92	1370
Middle	197	5	202
Secondary	72	13	85

College education has not spread much. There are only 11 colleges (government and private together) for general education. There is only one Industrial Training Institute in the entire district located in the Phulbani town.

HEALTH

The overall health scene in the district is particularly dismal, with only 37 beds available per one lakh population. There are nine hospitals, six dispensaries, thirty two primary health centers and three community health centers. The absence of adequate number of the first aid centres, medical aid centres and mobile health units (total 7 in number) indicates not only the lack of governmental initiative in the field of public health but also the low health consciousness among people.

VETERINARY CARE

There is now good scope for animal care as there is a fairly good number of dispensaries of veterinary services across the district. There are now adequate number of veterinary hospitals and dispensaries (a total of 18 together), live stock Aid centers (a total of 67) and Artificial Insemination Centers (a total of 31) (1993–94 figures).

POWER, COMMUNICATION ETC.

The drive for rural electrification is not in evidence. Barely 40 per cent of the villages have been electrified. Transport is mainly by road, since there are no railway lines running through the district territory. There are no National Highways passing through the district. Maximum road length is covered by Gram Panchayat roads (5311.70 *km)* followed by Panchayat Samiti roads (649.40 *km)*, the State Highways (369.60 *km)*, minor district roads (244.44 *km)* in the descending order. The number of banks and post offices per one lakh population is 8 and 48 respectively. The extension of telecommunication facility to the district in the last few years with 1152 subscribers in different parts marks a major step towards modernization.

WELFARE OF WEAKER SECTIONS

The weaker sections include the disadvantaged groups such as land less labour, holders of uneconomic farming units and village artisans. In the last one decade and a half poverty amelioration programmes have been vigorously undertaken. According to 1993–94 figures, 3493 beneficiaries have been covered under the Integrated Rural Development Programme. Besides, 169 houses have been constructed under the Indira Awas Yojana, 628 trained persons have been rehabilitated under TRYSEM, 639 wells have been dug under Jawahar Rojgar Yojana.

There is a good number of beneficiaries of the Integrated Tribal Development Programme in the area under TD Block of Phulbani covering the Alami Gram Panchayat. The table below shows the performance of ITDA, Phulbani in the decade between 1981–82 to 1991–92 which is quite remarkable, at times much ahead of its targets (See Table 2.2).

Table 2.2
Physical Achievement of the ITDA, Phulbani Between 1981-82 and 1991-92

Year	*Target*	*No. of Beneficiaries Assisted*
1981–82	Nil	52
1982–83	Nil	86
1983–84	250	116
1984–85	250	222
1985–86	115	80
1986–87	42	59
1987–88	150	136
1988–89	200	321
1989–90	200	214
1990–91	200	213
1991–92	200	214

INSTITUTIONS FINANCING DEVELOPMENT ACTIVITIES IN THE DISTRICT

There have been massive investments for development to the Kandhamal district during the 7th and 8th plan periods. The financial institutions making the investment include Scheduled Financial Corporation and NABARD, the OSCSTDFCC Limited etc.. The major financial institutions functioning in the district are as follows (See Table 2.3).

Table 2.3
Institutions Financing Development Activities in the Phulbani District

Sl. No.	*Name of the Financial Institutions*	*No. of Branches*
1.	State Bank	34
2.	United Commercial Bank	7
3.	Indian Bank	4
4.	Allahabad Bank	1
5.	Kalahandi Gramya Bank	15
6.	B.C.C. Bank	7
7.	O.S.F.C.	1
8.	CARD	1
Total		70

In order to facilitate smooth flow of credit, the District Credit Plan (DCP) has been prepared by the Branches on the basis of Village Credit Plan, made after a survey of villages allotted to them. In accordance with the DCP, credit is extended for schemes in the priority sector such as agricultural term loans, crop loans etc.. OSCSTDFCC Ltd. provides soft loans (marginal money Loans) to scheduled caste and scheduled tribe people under different anti-poverty programmes.

ECONOMIC INFRASTRUCTURE

The district is very badly handicapped as far the economic

infrastructure is concerned. This has an adverse impact on the smooth flow of credit. The banks have been providing credit in the face of mounting overdues which is against the capital adequacy norms and the income generation norms of these financial institutions. Besides, this has made the task of maintaining the desired transparency in the balance sheet of the banks extremely difficult.

The infrastructure constraints such as lack of communication, power supply and irrigation have affected the productivity of credit adversely. Lack of exposure to innovations in developmental mechanisms on the part of tribals has stood as an obstacle to the development of enterpreneurship in the district.

The incidence of poverty is acute in the district. Out of a total of 1,76,999 rural families, 1,59,275 families constituting 90 per cent of the total are under the poverty line. There are two ITDAs one each for Balliguda and Phulbani Sub-Division, working for the development of critical infrastructures as well as the promotion of income generating schemes for tribal families on the IRDP pattern. In certain areas, tribals continue to lead a very primitive life. The Kutia *Kandhas* are concentrated in some GPs of Tumudibandha block viz. Belghar, Guma, Lankagarh and Jhiripani and in the Subarnagiri area of Kotagarh Block. They practise slash and burn cultivation commonly known as *podu*. For uplift of this tribe, a micro project is implemented by the Kutia Kandha Development Authority which is functioning at Belghar.

THE OCCUPATIONAL STRUCTURE AND CHANGING PATTERN OF ECONOMIC ACTIVITIES

A vast majority of people of in the erstwhile Phulbani district belong to the agricultural families (88.9 per cent) and the rest are from families of wage labourers, traders and non-agricultural producers and government servants. Those belonging to agricultural families traditionally are either millet cultivators (South-West) or paddy cultivators (North and East). The millet cultivators exchange their produce of grams and pulses for low quality rice from the outside traders. The price of food grains usually comes down immediately after harvest and it shoots up before harvest.

Generally the price of rice is higher in the Kandhamals owing to the fact that, areas available for the cultivation are comparatively small and barren. Let us take the case of the Alami Gram Panchayat which is the focus of our study. There, out of a total of 1610 hectares only 524 hectares are cultivable land and the rest are uncultivated fallow land. The area of cultivation has increased only marginally, while there has been an unprecedented rise in the population of the district. As a result, price of rice has risen phenomenally over the years.

In fifty years time before independence, the price had gone up four times while in the last fifty years or so since independence, the price of rice has gone up 25 times. In 1896, one could buy 1.696 kg per one rupee while in 1946 with the same amount one could get 3.57 kg only and now in 1997 one gets less than 150 gms (133 grams approximately) per one rupee. Growing paddy being the main agricultural activity of the majority in the district, this inflationary trend pushed many people to look for sources of income other than agriculture. Added to this, cultivation was becoming highly unprofitable, forcing them to diversify into other areas. 1991 census corroborates this shift away. Out of the total population of 546281, there are 103000 cultivators, 74000 agricultural labourers, 48000 marginal (non-agricultural) workers. The non-workers are a huge 285000.

TRIBE-CASTE CONTINUUM

In the tribal areas of Orissa, the tribals and scheduled caste people live side by side. The relations between them are characterised by both cooperation and conflict. They are in need of each ot' er but their tie is seldom free from tension.

In the undivided Ganjam and Phulbani districts, the *Panas* happen to be the most numerous scheduled caste group. They live very close to the tribals either in a tribal village or at a little distance from it. The close and integral relationship between these two communities is symbolically expressed by the saying that, *the Panas* constitute the bark while the *Kandhas* represent the tree.

Tribal needs are both understood and taken advantage of by the *Panas* who originally were weavers. The fear of defilement which their lowly occupations generated, forced them to lead an arduous life in the different terrains of the agencies of south Orissa. They acted as interpreters to the *Kandhas,* who did not know the Oriya language. However, they are dubbed as a parasitic group, as they allegedly exploit *Kandhas* by taking advantage of the latter's innocence and ignorance.

In course of time, *Panas* along with other non-tribals took tribal lands into their possession paying a paltry sum in exchange. Some of the land less tribals were forced to work as hired labour by the fellow *Kandhas* or non-tribal Oriyas. Others changed their occupation to work as labourers in the non-farm sector i.e. construction of roads and buildings etc.

With the spread of education, the tribal access to new employment opportunities has been facilitated, the Tribals, both male and female, have taken up government jobs inside and outside the district. Security provided through reservation of jobs has motivated them to break away from the traditional occupational structure. However, in the domain of government service, the *Panas* have fared much better compared to the tribals. The more ambitious and the more dynamic among them have started taking up the career of a full time politician. Reservation of seats in the State and Central legislatures has given the tribals a significant voice in the respective political institutions. In the Orissa Vidhan Sabha, out of a total of one hundred and forty seven seats as many as thirty four seats have been reserved for the scheduled tribes which is a handsome 23.13 per cent of the total. While the Phulbani Lok Sabha seat is reserved for the scheduled caste, two of the three Assembly seats in the district are reserved for the scheduled tribe, the third one being reserved for the scheduled caste

Another factor responsible for the tribals' change of occupation is the practice of Goti, which originated from the indebtedness of tribals. Their lands were pledged to the money lenders for prolonged nonpayment of debts. Although there is a law prohibiting the debt bondage, the social condition did not practically permit a Goti to free himself from such bondage.

With the passage of time, the traditional beliefs of tribals are also undergoing change. The frequency of religious rites and ceremonies has been on the decline. As a result, there is a corresponding decline in the trading of sacrificial animals. *Panas* who used to have a bumper trade in buffalos have suffered an income squeeze in the process.

Furthermore, there has been progresive alienation of tribal land in course of time. This has forced a good number of tribals to work as wage labour. Wage payment is done in kind *(buti)* or cash *(mula)*. The agricultural labourers (the *halias)* are employed on annual contract for various agricultural operations such a sowing, weeding, harvesting, threshing etc. The *mulias,* belonging to the second category are paid their daily wage *(mula)* in cash.

The non-agricultural classes comprise persons including their dependents who earn their livelihood form sources other than cultivation. According to the 1971 census, non-agricultural workers were engaged in the following activities:

(1) livestock, forestry, fishing, hunting and plantations, orchards and allied activities (2) mining and quarrying (3) manufacturing, processing, servicing and repairs (household industry and others) (4) constructions (5) trade and commerce (6) transport, storage and communications and (7) other services.

Table 2.4(a)
Work Force Structure in the District Gender wise

Year	*Male Workers Out of Total Male Population*	*Female Workers Out of Total Female Population*	*Total Workers Out of Total Population*
1961	64.54%	48.35%	56.40%
1971	59.67%	10.99%	3335.29%

Table 2.4(b)
Occupation-wise Distribution of the Population of the District

Year	*Cultivators*	*Agriculture labourers*	*Residual workers*
1961	64. 19%	13.35%	22.46%
1971	55.16%	28.95%	15.89%

As far as women's occupations in the district are concerned the perception of the government has been the determining factor. In the 1971 census, there was a change in the definition of workers. In the 1961 census, housewives and students had been included as workers. But in the next census they were excluded from the category of workers. As a result, there was big drop in the number of workers in general and women workers in particular [See Table 2.4(a)]. Now-a-days the tribal women work as wage labour, if they have no work of their own. During "hungry seasons', they migrate to nearby work sites in search of some wage-based work. In the recent years some of the tribal women have gone into government service, while the more privileged of them have opted for political careers. Majority of them are still dependent on the government-sponsored schemes like DWACRA under IRDP, specially designed for them. Quite a few have started taking up vocations like tailoring for a livelihood with the help of District Rural Development Agency.

The supply of per capita agricultural land in the district is lowest in the state. What is more, the size of such land is shrinking everyday. The existing land for cultivation accounts for the livelihood of only a fragment of the population given the predominantly seasonal character of agriculture. The trend for most people has been to take up daily wage work as an additional means of livelihood to supplement the scanty income from the fields. They tend to combine farm and non-farm work depending on their need as well as availability of work opportunities. This gradual shift from farm sector to the non-farm sector has led to a change of the wage pattern in the Kandhamal district. Payment of wage in cash is gradually replacing the earlier mode of payment in kind. The wage rates are revised from time to time to match the price rise. Monetisation of the economy is clearly in evidence. In short, the spread of education, urbanisation, the growth in monetary transations and the developmental activities have contributed to their social as well as occupational mobility.

REFERENCE

1. Service Area Credit Plan 1994–95 — Background Paper for Phulbani and Boudh District prepared by LBO, Phulbani.

3

DEVELOPMENT PLANNING

CONCEPTS, APPROACHES AND EXPERIENCES

We do not merely live but continuously strive towards a better life. It is this striving which helps the societies to grow and evolve. Development involves rationalising our economic activities viz. the organisation and planning of production in particular. It may be agricultural production or industrial production depending on whether the society is in a pre-industrial revolution phase or in the post-industrial revolution phase. Development activities in a pre-industrial/an agrarian society are said to be in the pre-technology phase. This does not however preclude the application of technological innovations in the field of agricultural production. In a post-industrial society, development implies mass scale production and urbanisation; proliferation of industries and townships.

Rural Development is essentially a dichotomous concept. In one sense, it means urbanising the village and creating secondary and tertiary sectors, often, at the expense of the primary sector. In another sense, it implies infrastructural development, creation of work opportunities for the rural people etc. without destroying the spatial context. In the first sense, rural development underlines the rural urban dichotomy while in the latter sense, the underlying ideas are continuum and reciprocity. The latter approach is essential to integrated planning.

DEVELOPMENT AS GROWTH OF HUMAN SETTLEMENTS

Whatever may be the underlying idea, development refers to the developing of a human settlement where a group of people perform certain social and economic functions. A settlement system may be defined as a group of human settlements linked with each other functionally and otherwise. There are human and systemic components. While it is the human component which determines the fate of a settlement, the system as a whole plays a decisive role in determining the level of living and well-being of individual households and its members living therein. The physical aspects of their settlements include topography, natural resources etc. and the socio-economic aspects comprise economic opportunities and population growth which together determine the way these settlements evolve.

In India most of these settlements were rural settlements in the pre-industrial revolution phase with agriculture and related activites as the base. In the post-industrial revolution period, village became an agricultural production centre and the town, the industrial production and distribution centre. Technology brought in mass production. Villages remained stagnant while cities grew in functional complexity. Pressure of population on agriculture forced village people to migrate to cities in search of a living. Majority of them living in the villages remained marginalised in many ways, leading a life of poverty and deprivation.

GROWTH POLE APPROACH

Improvement in the conditions of the marginalised rural poor became the chief preoccupation of democratic governments world over. Poverty became a global concern. In India, rural development policies have been formulated from time to time to fight rural poverty and deprivation adopting different strategies. The main strategies are sectoral, spatial and decentralised planning. Those who follow the sectoral approach view rural development as a strategy to improve the socio-economic conditions of the poorer sections of the rural population such as the small scale farmers, tenants and the landless. According to a World Bank Sector Policy paper on rural development, it is a strategy designed to improve the economic and social life of a specific group of people. It involves extending the benefits of development to the poorest among those who seek a livelihood in the rural areas. The group includes small farmers, tenants and landless. It goes on to add "a national programme of rural development may be made up of single sector or multi-sector projects with components, implemented concurrently or in sequence. The components and phasing must be formulated both to remove constraints and to support those forces prevailing, on the target area which are favourable to development".

The spatial strategy of rural development on the other hand is premised on the theory that industrialisation and urbanisation of human settlements will lead to development of specific rural region benefits of which will percolate to the neighbouring areas. For example, the growth pole theory of development believes in creating certain industrial complexes as growth poles which will help benefits of development trickle down to the neighbouring areas. It will also help establish small town interdependencies to serve as hinterlands for the growth complexes. The growth pole hypothesis proved to be a failure since several newly established industrial complexes with inter-industry linkages failed to generate development in the surrounding rural region.

Another strategy[1] for the development of backward areas on similar lines is the *lead industry* strategy . A lead industry is expected to generate significant growth impulses and has high ability to innovate. It should be located in *developable* regions - places with growth potentials, so that it can exert a powerful pull effect on the *underdeveloped* regions of the world. In Orissa, for example, Natural Mineral Development Corporation Ltd., Birla group is the lead firm and the *developable* districts are Puri, Ganjam, Balasore, Mayurbhanja, Bolangir, Dehenkanal and Keonjhar. The exponents of the strategy opine that big business houses and successful large corporations in the public sector should be considered lead industries.

The strategy has two major flaws. Firstly, the lead industries have a tendency to convert themselves into "self sufficient and (self-dependent) enclaves and their relationship with other industries and areas is, more often than not, an exploitative one". Secondly, the cost of carrying out the strategy is much higher compared with an agriculture-oriented strategy.

GROWTH CENTRE APPRAOCH

In order to overcome the deficiencies in the *growth pole* approach, an integrated *growth centre* approach has been evolved, which provides for a hierarchical spatial arrangement. R.P. Mishra[2] an authority on regional planning has given a spatial model based on the *growth centre* concept. The model consists of 5 categories of *growth centres* i.e. (1) Development Poles (2) Development Centres (3) Development Points (4) Rural Service Centres and (5) Central Villages.

Central villages constitute the nuclei for services extending to about 6,000 population living in about 5 villages which are provided with marketing facilities, recreational facilities and social services.

Each *Rural Senvice Centre* will serve a population of 30,000. It has higher level functions than central villages and provides facilities for processing of agricultural products.

Each *Development Point* serves about 5 service centres and a micro-regional population of 150,000. It is predominantly an agro-industrial centre. Each *development, centre* will serve about 8 development points and a regional population of 1,20,000.

A *Development Pole* would serve about 20 million population. While the development centres specialized in secondary functions, the development pole specialized in tertiary functions.

Development planning in India has been, for the most part, sectoral. It has been elitist too. There is a heavy dependence on the governmental machinery in such planning as a consequence of which the realities of the situation are relegated to the background. Bureaucracy, in its broadest sense, is virtually the target group. In contrast, growth centre approach provides for spatial integration of all development activities with an interlinked system of strategic growth points. It is desirable that each sectoral investment in order to yield results, must be brought into the hierarchy of growth centres. This has the advantage of reducing bureaucratic elitism at various spatial levels. Sectoral planning is widely recognised as the most effective means of development although, as experience has shown, it results in uneven development . On the otherhand, spatial planning is useful for removing regional and district level imbalances.

Only from the Fourth Five Year Plan onwards, district planning became effective. The Planning Commission recommended that regional planning was to be done at the district level alongwith departmental co-ordination. The plan represented a major breakthrough in spatial planning. It gave priority to augmentation and rational allocation of resources for increasing productivity, improving distribution of incomes and reducing disparities between different areas and sections of the population. The plan objectives were realised successfully in the Punjab and in some pockets of Gujarat. The success was of course due to certain pre-existing factors such as the consolidation of land holdings of the earlier years, large investments in the water systems, provision of extension services from specialised institutions like Punjab Agricultural University etc. Further, the revolutionary potential of the new technology in the field of agriculture could be exploited successfully in the two states.

Experts suggested that this could be extended to areas like animal husbandry, industry and energy. New credit agencies were established with financial and technical sinews, not known before. There was a 'synergistic' effect in harnessing all this potential in an integrated fashion.

Drawing inspiration from the Punjab experiment in agricultural innovations, A.D. Moodie[3], a rural development expert has devised a model for rural development synergy based on the new awareness and appreciation of science and technology of their potentials in all aspects of rural development and their application to the potentials of nature, of the infrastructure, and of the human factor through various managerial and social techniques.

The science and technology potentials are applied to the potentials of nature, of the infrastructure and of the human factor through land, water and energy resources, through live stock management, through growth centres, and through rural populations uplifted from poverty and enriched with community care health plans and new designs for more relevant education to enhance the quality of rural life. All these point to calculations of financial needs and appropriate financing agencies such as the state exchequer, the commercial banks, agricultural finance and co-operative credit organisation with new innovative organisational experiments reaching out to the small farmer and the landless labourers. The arrows in the above chart indicate the synergy flows and interactions of all these potential and factors.

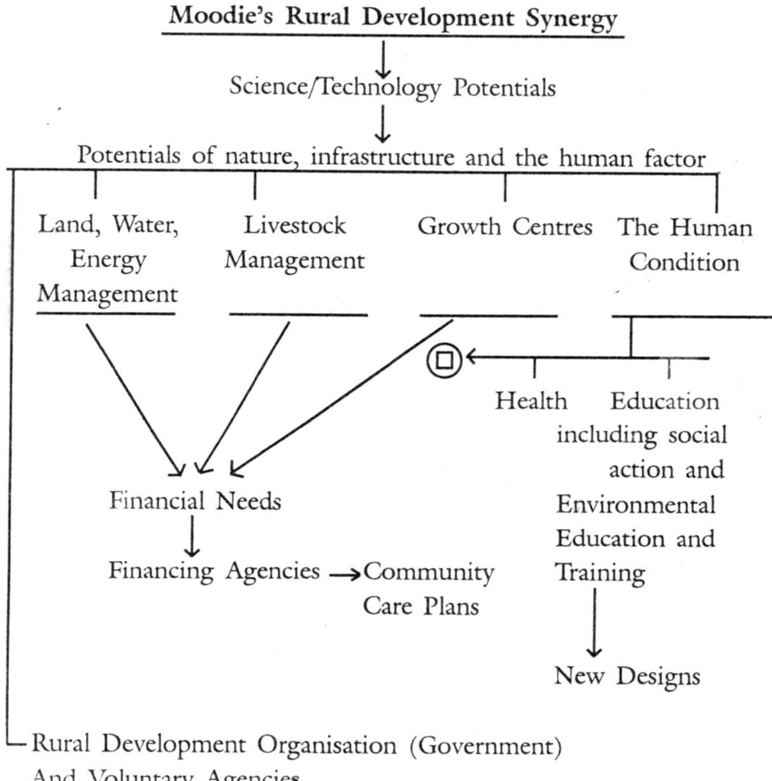

Organisational innovations become necessary to blend the roles of local officials, technical specialists and local leaders for best management of micro plans. Further as A.D. Moodie has suggested, there should be a new district planner based on the availability of the advanced technologies in ecology, hydrology, agronomy, livestock, fisheries, forest management, social science planning and managerial economics.

Rural development synergy requires a high degree of motivation and movement of individuals and local communities. It also requires a great deal of local initiative in the form of dynamic local leadership capable of adapting to new technologies, accommodating new patterns of business which integrate rural areas of the country with national market. The public sector is expected to extend infrastructure, provide growth centre where training and educational facilities are concentrated without taking over the existing trade functions. It must make provision for employment to those who remain outside the competitive market economy.

Rural demand must be stimulated through agricultural development by raising rural incomes by techniques of efficient investment (with low capital/out put ratio) by providing rural employment both of a viable and compassionate nature. The growth centre programme must be activated in areas where the physical criteria for such programme is available adopting the following methods.

In order to augment agricultural productivity, there must be provision of positive credit which enables the user to produce net surplus above cost. It also enables people to modernise the economic enterprise and raise their living standard. Credit is a scarce resource and there must be a strategy to utilise credit in such a way that it will, at a given level of investment, result in increasing production. It should be utilised to upgrade technology and increase operational efficiency. Rationality demands that it must revolve as many times as possible within a given period. Credit should be converted into agro services, wherever necessary. Most importantly, a rational credit provision must result in bridging the gap between the large and small farmers as well as in creating additional employment potential.

The practice of credit utilisation in the last three decades or so shows that the large and medium size farmers have availed themselves of credit facilities from co-operatives to multiply acreages by the scales of finance. This implies that large farmers get substantial amount of money as cultivation expenses which they do not in fact need. Further, in calculating the amount required by these farmers, the incremental income resulting from the investments already made in agriculture has never been taken into consideration viz. in terms of ploughback of resources formation by the beneficiary farmers.

There is a need, therefore, to bridge the gap between the big farmers and the small farmers by taking into account the surplus accruing to the big farmer while computing his demand thereby reducing the needs of big farmers for credit substantially. This in effect, will leave a sizeable fund with the institutional agencies for financing programmes of small farmers, marginal farmers, oral lessee, share croppers rural artisans, tribals etc. Continuous innovations as regards financing, as cited above, certainly constitutes an important ingredient of development. Nevertheless, the basis of development banking must be followed: (1) One, the loans will have to be production-oriented, incremental income generating and consequently self-liquidation (2) Two, institutional finance must be made available to the weaker sections in assisting them to achieve a state of viability. The chief sources of agricultural credit in India are money-lenders, co-opertives, commercial banks, direct finance by the Government in the shape of Taccavi and specialised agencies like Agricultural Refinance Corporation, Rural Electrification Corporation etc.

The Green Revolution no doubt changed the face of Indian agriculture radically in the form of technological innovations, expansion of irrigation facilities etc. But in the process, it not only created wide disparities in the ranks of the framers but it also made the small farmers more and more insecure and vulnerable. The Fifth Five Year Plan sought to remedy the situation while laying out the basic objectives of national plan which included (a) maximum institutionalization of credit, (b) a substantial flow of institutional credit to small farmers and other weaker section of the society, (c) reduction in regional imbalances in the provision of national credit. The plan extended certain concessions and safeguards, too, for the weaker sections, without compromising substantially the goal of productivity.

(*a*) by favouring production-oriented rather than security-oriented lending.

(*b*) by giving priority to small cultivators, if total resources are limited.

(*c*) by entrusting cooperatives with the task of collecting share capital from small cultivators.

(*d*) by fixing separate credit limits for them.

(*e*) by liberalising evaluation of security loans.

(*f*) by issuing joint loans for small farmer groups.

MARKETING APPROACH

It is about the Fifth Plan period that Indian agriculture began to acquire a competitive character and marketing was recognised as a very important dimension of a competitive economy. Gradually, there was greater external demand for local products which implied more job opportunities for those engaged in agriculture, agro-business, handicrafts, extention services etc. There was no need to create a demand for articles of daily use in the rural areas such as kerosene, soap, cigarettes, as there were large companies already. But for the local products of quality which can be sold outside at a high value, there was a need not only to generate demand but also to advertise and market them through public sector undertakings. To quote Paul Hoffman (address to the UNDP in 1972) "Our illusion is that you can industrialise a country by building factories. You do not. You industrialise it by building markets". In short, marketing is the quintessence of industrialisation.

The marketing approach adopted in our country to protect and promote village and small industries was sought to be extended to rural development. The Khadi and Village

Industries Commission (KVIC), the National Small and Village Industries Commission (NSIC) pursued the objective at the national level. At the state level, the Maharashtra Agro Development and Fertiliser Corporation Ltd. (MAFCO) of Maharashtra and Amul Diary of Kheda district of the same state can be cited as some examples of marketing strategy. The KVIC looked after Khadi and 22 village industries such as handicrafts, handloom, coir silk, seri-culture and small industries. Among the agro-products which were marketed by KVIC were cane gur, khandsari, groundnut oil, cereals and pulses, leather, palm gur etc. The NSIC was responsible for the marketing of specialised products from specific rural areas with a view to getting better returns and also with a view to improving the quality of products. In the field of diary industry, Amul Diary stands out as a bright example of successful marketing.

There are instances of application of this approach in the field of rural crafts also. The Maharashtra State Khadi and Village Industry Board in consultation with the State Government and Reserve Bank of India provided credit to the rural artisans engaged in the village industries such as leather, fibre, carpentry and black smithing, cane and bamboo, processing of cereals, oil, pulses and wool. This was done in response to the Planning Commission's concern for the gradual disappearance of the artisans of the village. The other objective was to give a fillip to the marketing of the village craft goods inside the country as well as abroad for which the Commission encouraged launching of new schemes.

Bank financing was extended to the tribals of the Ambegaon Taluka in Poona district to supplement their income by collecting mirabolams which sold at Rs. 50 per quintal. Similar steps were taken by the Maharashtra government to engage a nomadic tribe of Wadar in the excavation work in the Kukdi Irrigation Project in Poona district.

The above discussion on the productive use of credit, demand generation and marketing of goods and services clearly point towards the entry of market capitalism in the rural sector. At the same time, the recognisation of the need to protect the weaker sections which become vulnerable in the work of agricultural modernisation point to the contrary need of the presence of a 'hard' state. The two imperatives of development (a) of ensuring growth and (b) ensuring social justice are conceptually incongruous and therefore, difficult to combine. Market capitalism requires that, the role of the state should be minimal. Therefore, there is a need to have strategic organisations to make development planning socially effective.

ORGANISATIONAL APPROACH

Ideas are realised through organisations. Planning takes a concrete shape only when it is implemented through certain agencies/organisations. Three types of organisations with separate functions have been recommended to make the process of development effective. They are (i) *apex* organisation which monitor development (ii) *spearhead*, organisation which think development (iii) *action* organisation which actually implement plans of development. A good organisational plan is necessary to effectively implement and supervise projects and to recover the loans. The developmental organisations have to work in collaboration with the extension departments of the State governments. There should be a core group to act as the spearhead organisation comprising the Development Commissioner, Agricultural Production Commissioner, Secretary (Irrigation), Director of Agriculture and Chairman of the State Electricity Board to review implementation of integrated projects. At the action level, we should have the district personnel entrusted with the implementation of development schemes. They are the (1) the Collector (2) the

Sub-Divisional Officer (3) the District Development Officer (4) the District Panchayat Officer (5) the Block Development Officers (6) the Block Extension Officers and finally (7) the Village Level Workers. At the grass root level, there are officials like the Sarpanch, the Secretary of the Gram Panchayat, who are responsible for the implementation of programmes at the village level. In the Second Five Year Plan which introduced district planning demarcated clearly the development activities of the Centre, the State and the District. However, the idea of district planning came into operation only during the Fourth Five Year Plan period. The Fifth Five Year Plan marked a definite improvement in the concept of organisation. Regional planning was introduced with special reference to tribal development and tribal sub-plans were prepared towards this end.

The plan also envisaged micro-level planning for basic planning units. Growth centers were sought to be created to ensure development along with cultural integration. It also provided for multi-level planning—*micro, meso* and *macro* levels with functional linkages between planning units at all the levels. At the *micro* level, the project area was to be coterminus with administrative boundaries covering one or more full tahasils. At the *meso* level, the project area comprised contiguous blocks. *Macro* level consisted of two or more projects. The plan laid emphasis on spatial integration and special approaches.

For instance, the Madras Institute of Development Studies prepared a plan for restructuring of the spatial pattern of the Bastar community. It is a five-tier system comprising 89 central villages, 30 service towns, 7 market towns, 3 growth points and 2 growth centres. Another study made by National Institute of Rural Development Studies, Hyderabad recommended a plan for integrated tribal development of Keonjhar district of Orissa. It prescribes a four-tier system in the spatial frame comprising dependent villages, central villages, service towns and growth centres.

In order to apply the growth models of this kind the existing politico-administrative setup is considered inadequate. There is a proposal to create a special authority. Since growth involves coordination of a large number of complex functions, it is unlikely that the Central and State governments can carry out the job effectively. Therefore, it is proposed that a separate authority called Authority for Backward Area Development (ABAD) should be created.

Such an organisation, it is suggested, should lay emphasis on social diffusion process. Besides, backward states and backward areas must be adequately represented on its body and there should be emphasis on rural-urban linkage and rural development in the ABAD's programme.

NATIONAL PROGRAMME OF DEVELOPMENT

Experiments and Experiences

Regional disparities which were caused due to the uneven impact of British colonialism persisted in the Post Independence period and stood as stumbling blocks in the path of equitable development. The green revolution further aggravated the disparities by strengthening the rich farmers. There was overall growth in the GDP, per capital income although the economically deprived sections continued to be further impoverished. Agricultural growth with the use of new technology, HYV seeds, fertilizers etc. in certain regions gave rise to a class of *nouveau riches.* The disparities deepened as the democratic goals of distributive justice and social equality drifted compelling a change of focus in economic planning towards the end of the 1960s.

Before the Fourth Five Year Plan, the stress was on land reforms, community development programmes, cooperative farming. During the Fourth Plan period which is described as the "technology investment phase", efforts were made to meet the food crisis and augment food production by leaps and bounds. Neither of the two strategies could truly develop the rural society, especially the masses of the rural unemployed poor. In the 1970s and 1980s there came a shift of emphasis in rural development strategy from agricultural growth to the betterment of the poor. During the 1970s, special agriculture and employment programmes for the weaker sections were initiated on a national scale. Some of them were area-specific programmes while others were group specific programmes. Among the area-specific programmes, we have DPAP, IADP, DDP, HADP, TADP etc. and in the category of group specific programmes, we have programmes for target groups like Small farmers (SFDA), Marginal Farmers (MFAL) and Tribals (ITDP) etc.

The SFDA was created in 1969-70, on the recommendation of the report of the All India Rural Credit Review Committee. Its objective was to ensure the viability of the small farmer. It was to act at the district level as a catalyst agency in identifying small farmers, investigating their problems and ensuring supply of inputs from various developmental organisation . It was to act through the existing agencies to the maximum extent possible.

The MFAL was launched in the same year with the objective of improving the productivity of farmers' land and pursuing related activities such as animal husbandry, dairying etc.. In the initial year, it was to be kept separate from the SFDA since it was to act as a catalyst for development of marginal farmers with an all India coverage. After a couple of years however, MFAL was merged in the SFDA.

The Rural Works Programme was launched in 1970–71 in 54 districts with a view to generating employment through the execution of rural works. The programme was later reoriented to follow the area development approach. It became a complete scheme following the mid-term appraisal of the 4th Plan and renamed as Drought Prone Area Programme. The programme aimed at (a) restoration of ecological balance (b) integrated area development (c) equitable distribution of development benefits (d) generation of employment. By 1980, 74 districts covering 13 states were covered under this programme.

The fight against rural unemployment was carried forward through the introduction of Crash Scheme for Rural Employment (CSRE) which was operational between 1971 and 1974. The basic objectives of the programme were generation of employment in all districts at the rate of 2.5 lakh mandays per annum in each district and creation of durable assets in consonance with local development plan. The scheme was simultaneously administered by the department of rural development of the centre and department of panchayat development of the state. A hundred per cent grants-in-aid efforts by the centre led to the creation of 3160 lakh mandays of employment. Under the programme, important steps were taken in the areas of road construction, land development and minor irrigation. The block development agencies and the Panchayat Raj Institutions were the primary implementers of the programme.

Tribal Areas Development Programme initiated during the Fifth Five Year Plan was an area specific programme with special focus on the development of the tribal population. The programme was operational in the tribal sub-plan areas which were divided into 180 tribal development projects. The broad objectives of the Tribal Sub-Plan were two : (i) to narrow the gap between tribals and non-tribals (ii) to end exploitation of tribals in the areas of liquor vending, land alienation, money lending and collection of forest produce. Tribal Development Corporations were established to provide an integrated credit-*cum*-marketing service to the tribals. The programmes under the Tribal Sub-Plan were supported by the sectoral outlays in the state plans. Besides, institutional finance was available for selected programmes.

The Minimum Needs Programme which was also launched during the Fifth Five Year Plan aimed at providing a minimum level of physical and social infrastructures in the countryside. It sought to combine and integrate social consumption programmes with economic development programmes. The programme had social components such as elementary education, rural health, rural water supply, rural roads, rural electrification, housing sites for landless labourers, environmental improvement of slums and nutrition. The emphasis of the programme was to accelerate growth in consonance with the social objectives of the plan.

The National Rural Employment Programme (NREP) introduced during the Sixth Five Year Plan had three major objectives: (i) generation of employment for the unemployed and the under employed men and women in the rural areas (ii) strengthening of the rural infrastructure leading to rapid growth of rural economy and raising the income of the rural poor and (iii) raising of the nutritional status and living standard.

The Integrated Approach to Rural Development (IRDP) which was operational from the Sixth Five Year Plan onwards was probably the most successful of all development experiments so far. The programme was launched at the block level on a limited scale in 1978–79. Later it was extended to all the blocks, the total numbering 5011, The objective of the programme was to generate assets and employment opportunities to the rural poor to enable them to rise above the poverty line. Its target group consisted of the poorest of the rural poor, small and marginal farmers, agricultural and non-agricultural labourers, rural artisans and craftsmen, scheduled caste and scheduled tribe families who live below the poverty line. Special priority to the SC and ST families was accorded under the programme by extending to them 30% of the subsidies and loans. The programme was comprehensive in as much as it combined the package approach, the target group concept, the cluster approach of the CAD (Command Area Development) type and the antyodaya concept.

IMPLEMENTATION OF PROGRAMMES: THE TRENDS ACROSS THE NATION

In the course of the implementation of the development programmes, one could notice a few clear trends. For example, the programmes related to the traditional occupational structure yielded beneficial results. Facilities for marketing the surplus have given a boost to the size of the occupational structure and consequently raised the living standards. One RBI study (1975) of the Small Farmer Development Agencies concluded that, the schemes like poultry, piggery, sheep breeding were best supported when they were taken up by the traditional occupational groups associated with animal husbandry activities.

Another trend was that the creation of specialised agencies like the SFDA facilitated the viability of the target population in different areas. One may cite two case studies of small and marginal farmers of Himachal Pradesh by Maitra[4] and Kingra[5]. In this regard, Maitra has shown how the SFDA working there succeeded in organising landless agricultural labourers into a vegetable estate which secured the "release" of labourers from rich cultivators and how it adopted a mixed farming system to suit the environment and covered risks of failure. According to Kingra, The SF and MF had very small holdings in the hilly conditions of Himachal Pradesh.

Thirdly, the programmes providing necessary linkages were quite successful. The SFDA beneficiaries in the state, as

Maitra's study has shown, were given land on lease, credit and marketing support as a result of which the schemes could be successfully implemented. The RBI study of 1975 supports such package approach for the animal husbandry programmes, particularly for dairying. Another study of the Tamilnadu Poultry Development Corporation scheme in Chinglepet district of Tamil Nadu (1978) by the Project Monitoring and Evaluation Cell of the Syndicate Bank which financed the scheme has shown the usefulness of the integrated approach of providing all inputs such as chicks, equipment, feed, veterinary care etc. to the beneficiary farmers. According to the findings of the study, the linking of credit with marketing is the most important factor for the improved economic status of the beneficiary farmers, marginal and small.

With regard to employment generation, reports of the Project Evaluation Organisation of the Planning Commission offer some valuable insights. The report of the PEO[6] about the Food and Work Programme conducted in 10 districts in 1979 showed that 70% of the 793 beneficiaries received daily or weekly payment rather than fortnightly or monthly wage. The response of the government to the report was positive. The programme was modified to provide continual rather than short-term employment. However, implementation of the modified programme, as the report assessed, resulted in the exclusion of the landless agricultural labourers from the Employment Guarantee Scheme as there was no provision for daily payment. It may be noted that the poorest require year- round work and not seasonal work.

An earlier report of the PEO[7] had shown that the non-farm labour specified "work not suitable" as one of the reason for their non-participation in the employment programme. The programme under study was the Crash Scheme for Rural Employment. It was inferred by the study group that, the group interviewed was possibly a skilled group which was not attracted to unskilled or manual labour. But generally speaking, the focus of public works programmes such as FFP, CSRE and Employment Guarantee Scheme (EGS) was right in the sense that the service offered under these programmes was of a simple nature involving little skill and benefited the weaker sections the most. It may also be pointed out that the recruitment of village level workers from among the beneficiaries helps reduce the complexities of service. Likewise, in the area of health, the recruitment of the Community Health volunteers has reportedly been of immense help in extending health care service to the rural families[8].

PROBLEMS AND SHORTCOMINGS

In spite of some success of the late 70s, the implementation of programmes is handicapped by several problems, some of which are owing to faulty planning while there are a few others arising at the field level.

At the planning level, it is necessary to have specific delineation of beneficiary groups such as leather workers, sheep breeders etc. which makes them more homogeneous and identifiable categories than labels such as the poor/weaker sections, small/marginal farmers, peasants, tribals etc.. Lack of clarity in this respect leads to problems. For instance, the so-called 'small farmer' group was found to be a heterogeneous mix of marginal, small and big farmers, when judged according to the non-farm income standards[9]. The Antyodaya programme overcame this problem of beneficiary identification very successfully through a participative camp approach[10,11&12]. Camps were organised to identify beneficiary households through Gram Sabha gatherings. Revenue camps were held to distribute benefits such as land and pension, similarly credit camps were held to ensure distribution of credit.

Secondly, the benefits of development have hardly reached the poorest among the beneficiaries. It has been commented by many critics that the HYV seeds and related inputs were offered to the farming community at large but the benefits were appropriated by the relatively more resource endowed.[13&14]

Thirdly, it has been pointed out that the lack of effective extension services blocks the entry of weaker sections into the club of the privileged. According to the RBI (1975), SFDA's dependence on the field level organisation of government in the distribution of credit was wrong. Further, the agency's focus on subsidy distribution rather than facilitation made it rather ineffective[15]. Yet another study of the working of the SFDA by Madras Institute of Development studies"[16] in 1980 revealed how the institutional norms have stood in the way of effective implementation of schemes. It pointed out that, the insistence on land as security over and above the hypothecation of assets arising out of the loan excluded the landless sections for whom benefits such as bullock carts, sheep units etc. were most appropriate.

Technology does not always serve as a positive factor of development. It, too, can be a barrier against broad-based development. Access to programme service depends on the nature of technology. For instance, it has been shown in a study relating to subsidy on the investment for a bio-gas plant that the less well-off groups cannot have free land to install the plant and water for mixing the dung.[17]

There are practical field problems even with regard to participation approach in the identification of beneficiaries. For example, the act of presenting oneself as a tenant farmer would invite the wrath of the local land owner.[18] The same problem is encountered while clinching oral leasing agreements.[19]

Finally, there is the cultural barrier to development. The norms of culture are, often, at variance with those of development. For instance, the concept of wage employment is alien to the Hindus who view work as service and, not as exchange. Further, there is an ascriptive dimension to poverty. Poverty is attributed to birth and fate. In reality, however, much of the benefit does not actually reach the poor due to the intervention of unscrupulous officials and middlemen. Further, whatever little reaches them is not put to much use since they are resigned and lack the motivation to grow. Another normative requirement, for the Hindus, to keep the aspiration level at the minimum goes against basic assumptions of development—a will to grow and an enterprising nature. Moreover, the presence of strong notion of 'community' among rural people slows down the process of development. To quote A.F. Barnbas decisions are often made on the basis of precedents rather than on rational choice. Since the importance of community is very high, an individual tends to take decision on how he perceives the community would react rather than on the basis of merits of alternate choice. Pointing at the mismatch between the values of Indian people and the modernization process, he says "while these values can be meaningful and useful for society, they can also slow down the process of directed change. Prominent among the values necessary for modernization to become operational in rural areas are interest in the present and the future rather than in the past, a disposition to accept new ideas, faith in science and technology, concepts of planning, organisation and efficiency".

Based on the reports and observations on development activities it may be pointed out (i) that there is a multiplicity of most programmes (ii) that many programmes have been operational for too short a duration to make an impact (iii) that some of the programmes have been continued after repeated failures leading to mindless squandering of public funds (iv) that, seen from the national angle, the extent of 'real' help that reached the poor was much less than the official figures make us believe (v) that, there is no necessary one-to-one relationship between development policy and the intended social outcome (vi) that, the rigidity of the social structure and cultural orientations of village people constitute the socio-psychological counterpoints to development (vii) that, there is lack of a truly participative process in the country as a whole.

DECENTRALISED PLANNING

The failure of centralised planning pointed to the need to adopt a participatory approach to development. There was emphasis on people-oriented development rather than achievement of physical targets only. Experience has shown that participation, direct and indirect was necessary in sustaining any programme. Realising this, the Sixth Five Year Plan took up the issue of beneficiary participation, more than the previous plans. As a result, indirect participation through voluntary organisations, local groups and panchayats acquired great importance in the implementation of programmes thus ushering the country into an era of decentralised planning.

Decentralised Planning constitutes an important part of the integrated approach to development which is popular in many parts of the world. For instance, the regional development projects in Afghanistan (PACCA), Ethiopia (CADU), Mexico (PUEBLA) are based on the integrated approach. The relative superiority of this approach vis-a-vis other approaches lies in the fact that it seeks to blend the perspective of growth with that of social equality. In the words of Koetter (1974) "the two operational targets of integrated rural development are equitable access to resources and distribution of benefits from development and a more equitable distribution of power, which requires the participation of more and more people at more and more levels, not only in the execution of developmental activities but also in the decision-making process.

Another reason accounting for its superiority over other approaches is that it is a package approach "a package of improved practices, largely technological improvements plus extension, credit and marketing for the promotion of agricultural production". In India, this has found its first programmatic expression in the intensive agricultural district programme.

But the integrated approach as the planning approach has one important limitation. Targets are set by national bodies but the emphasis is on the regional level with respect to decision-making and implementation. This weakens the position of the central administration and the planning authorities. According to one critic, the approach assumes that decentralised planning can achieve better mobilisation of local resources and equitable participation of all rural groups and social classes on the basis of the existing local administrative structure.[20]

On a practical plane, however, the organisational sphere has the inherent problem of integration. Moreover, participation is likely to create a privileged class since local organisations are likely to serve minority rather than majority needs. The policy makers are, therefore, caught in the dilemma between efficiency and equity objectives. Given the problem of incompatibility between integration and decentralisation we may suggest that planning should be done at the district level. Besides, there must be an articulation of political will behind the programme before it is implemented in order that decentralized planning becomes compatible with development plans and targets set by the higher levels of authority. Lastly, a word of caution with regard to participation may not be out of place. Participation may mean different thing. It may imply the involvement of more or other institutions; it may mean involvement of more services or staff as far as execution of development scheme is concerned. It may also imply participation of the people who are target groups of development. Von Blackenburg has expressed apprehension that participation may create regional inequalities depending on the degree and intensity of participation in different regions.[21]

POVERTY MEASUREMENT: METHODS

Whatever is the approach to planning development, the basic objective of development across the world remains the same—the eradication of poverty. Poverty has become an international concern, though what constitutes poverty is country-specific. The moot question, however, is, how to measure poverty. It is the method of measuring poverty which helps define the economic policy of a nation. There are two internationally recognised methods to do so. One is the poverty line (PL) method and the other, the Unsatisfied Basic Needs (UBN) method.

World Development Report adopts the poverty line method and treats the income—poor as poor. According to the report, the poor are heterogeneous and the main sources of their income are agriculture and sale of labour (the latter includes both rural and urban labour). The report further maintains that poverty is greater in rural areas than in urban areas. Poverty line refers to a quantitative 'threshold' which, according to the report, rises slowly at low levels of average consumption but more sharply at higher levels. It uses one type of poverty line for measuring poverty within countries and another—international poverty line, for global poverty estimates.

The UBN method is a direct method which measures poverty not as a quantitative phenomenon but as a qualitative one. In Latin American countries, both the methods PL and UBN have been applied to assess poverty.[22] Elsewhere also, one finds simultaneous application of both. The similarities and differences between the two methods are as follows :

PL method is characterized by	*UBN method is characterized by*
1. Definition of basic needs and their satisfiers	1. Definition of basic needs and their satisfiers
2. Definition of standard basket of satisfiers (SBES) for each household	2. Selection of variables and indicators that, for each need and satisfier express their degree of satisfaction
3. Cost of estimation of the SBES which makes up the poverty line	3. Definition of a minimum level for each indicator below which the need is considered unsatisfied
4. Classification of households whose income or consumption is below the PL, as poor	4. Classification of households as poor when one or more basic need(s) are unsatisfied
5. Comparision of the poverty line with household income (or consumption)	

One major shortcoming of the poverty line method is that each member of a poor household is considered poor. As a result, there is a problem of translating information on household consumption into information on individual consumption. Simply by dividing total consumption by the number of adult equivalents in a household we are bound to ignore the problem of intra-household inequality since the needs of the members are so different. Another shortcoming of the PL method is that the head-count index which is used cannot emphasize the depth of poverty.

ALTERNATIVE INDICATORS OF DEVELOPMENT

Corresponding to the two different methods of poverty, there are two alternative indicators of development. Gross Domestic Product and the Social Progress Index. Per capita

GDP may be defined as an approximation to the average amount of welfare means available in a given year. Any development indicator should reveal what GDP reveals; how far a society has departed from the realm of scarcity into the realm of abundance[23].

The success of the GDP as the development indicator is largely due to the weaknesses of the alternative approach which are as follows:

1. Social Progress Index is usually expressed in artificial units and not in figures.
2. With regard to its conceptual framework, it is not always explicitly formulated.
3. It dose not generate the same degree of consensus.

The limitations of the GDP are:

1. It records those welfare means which can be transacted in the market, leaving aside, among others all good and services produced by domestic work.
2. Conversely, it records commodities such as weapons and cigarettes which can hardly be considered means of welfare.
3. The prices of goods and services reflect all the biases of the markets, including externalities.
4. In referring only to one period, it does not take into account interdependencies over time nor does it reflect socially accumulated welfare means.
5. It does not take into account the social distribution of achievement means.
6. It does not account for educational levels and skills, nor free time for education or recreation which are welfare means.

Social Progress Index emphasizes quality of life and measures welfare in terms of opportunity and achievement. Level of welfare depends on the efficiency of the system, in transforming the opportunities (or means) into human welfare. Those societies which dedicate a higher percentage of their welfare means to basic goods and services (food, education, health care, housing, basic sanitation etc) most certainly will have higher levels of welfare as a result of their greater efficiency in transforming opportunities into welfare, While adopting the social progress index to assess development, it should be ensured that the opportunity set (built at the macro social level) and the achievement set (built mainly at the micro level) should be expressed in measurement units handled by the population in every day life thus making its general adoption easy.

The World Development Report (1990) concentrates on three key social indicators under-five mortality, life expectancy and net primary school enrolment rate, apart from income/consumption poverty. The human development report (1990), on the other hand adopts the Social Progress Index solely. Yet, there is much similarity in the observations made in the two reports. The two reports are unanimous on the quantitative magnitude of poverty in developing countries. Both agree that, during the 1960s and 1970s, the poor improved their position as regards both consumption and social indicators. In the words of Ravi Kanbur, the two reports agree on the fundamentals. Poverty alleviation requires growth but growth is not enough. The growth must be broad based and labour-intensive, and it must go hand in hand with purposive and targeted basic social expenditures.[24]

DEVELOPMENT AND STRUCTURAL ADJUSTMENT

Towards the beginning of the 1990s the nature of state intervention began to change radically due to grave financial crisis in many countries and the developmental activities in these countries had to be sustained through increased capital flows from the developed countries. Describing the 1980s as a lost decade, the international agencies asked the developing countries to have development policies by restructuring their economies. This is popularly known as structural adjustment which involved substantial loss of political sovereignty by the developing nations vis-a-vis the capitalist countries. Policy-guidelines were given to the 'adjusting' countries suffering a decline in government expenditures and in per capita incomes. They were instructed to have low-cost programmes to keep down the across-the-board interventions and to rely more on targeted schemes.[25] Furthermore, they were to run programmes having social safety nets for the poor i.e. income transfer programmes etc. They were also to adopt public employment schemes which would act as a safety net against the vagaries of agrarian production. International finance was to be made available to sustain these schemes.

Briefly speaking, the policy of structural adjustment underlined the need, on the part of 'adjusting' countries, to reduce demand for imports by strengthening dependence on domestic goods to stabilise economic conditions and the need to restructure their economies to reach a higher growth path.[26] These countries had to accept international monitoring of their development activities, surrendering a substantial part of their political sovereignty. This policy has been criticized as a 'neo-colonial game-plan' of the international capitalist regime seeking global legitimization under the pretext of removing global poverty.

REFERENCES

1. A.V. Srinivasan, "Lead Industry Strategy for Developing Backward Areas" First IFCI lecture delivered under the auspices of Faculty of Management Studies, University of Delhi on March, 1978.
2. R.P. Mishra, "Growth Centres and Rural Urban Continium" in AD. Moodie, ed., *Approaches to Rural Development* (Mumbai 1976), pp. 49–65.

3. A.D. Moodie, ed., *Approaches to Rural Development* (Mumbai, 1976).
4. D.K. Maitra, "Experiences in Organising Economic Activities" in B.M. Desai ed. *Intervention for Rural Development* (Ahmedabad, IIM, 1977).
5. I.S. Kingra , "Performance of SFDA and its programmes, Sirmur District, Himanchal Pradesh In B.M. Desai, ed., *Intervention for Rural Development—Experiences of the Small Farmers Development Agency* (Ahmedabad, Indian Institute of Management, 1977).
6. Programme Evaluation Organisations, "Evaluation Report" (1980a) of Food for Work Programme—August–October 1979, (New Delhi) 1980.
7. Programme Evaluation Organisations, "Report (1979c) of Study for Crash Scheme for Rural Employment—1971–74, 1979.
8. National Institute of Health and Family Welfare, "An Evaluation of Community Health Workers," *NIHFW Reports* (New Delhi) 1978 & 1979.
9. Reserve Bank of India, "The Small Farmers Development Agencies — A Field Study" *RBI Report* (Murnbai) 1975.
10. M.L. Mehta, "Partners in Development" (New Delhi'), Centre for Policy Research Paper Presented at the *Seminar on Poverty. Population and Hope,* Pune, 1981.
11 A. Mukharjee and N. Sengupta, "Rajasthan's Antyodaya Programme", *Yojana,* April 1979.
12. I. Khana & A. Subramanium, "Learning from Antyodaya—some lessons for IRDF" (Ahmedabad) Indian Institute of Management, Working Paper No. 426, 1982.
13. Francine R. Frankel, *India's Green Revolution—Economic Gains and Political Costs* (Princeton, Princeton University, 1971).
14. F. Tummason Jannuzi, *Agrarian Crisis In India—The Case of Bihar* (Mumbai, Sangam, 1974).
15. B.M. Desai, ed, *Intervention for Rural Development — Experiences of the Small Farmers Development Agency* (Ahmedabad, Indian Institute of Management, 1977).

16. Madras Institute of Development Studies "Structure and Intervention — An Evaluation of DAAP. IRDP and Related Programmes in Ramanathpuram and Dharampuri District of Tamil Nadu" (Madras, MIDS, 1980).
17. T.K. Moulik and Others. " Biogas System in India — A Socio Economic Evaluation", (Ahmedabad), An Indian Institute of Management Paper, 1978.
18. Ashok Rudra, " One Step Forward, Two Steps Backward", *Economic and Political Weekly* (Mumbai), Vol. XVI, No. 25–26, 1981.
19. Francine, R. Frankel, *India's Political Economy : 1947–1977* — The Gradual Revolution (Delhi. Oxford University Press, 1978).
20. See Peter Von Blackenburg, "Organisational Aspects of Mobilisation of People in Integrated Rural Development" in Ajit K. Danda, ed., *Studies on Rural Development — Experiences and Issues* (New Delhi, Inter-India, 1984).
21. *Ibid,*
22. See Julio Boltvinik, "Poverty Measurement and Alternative Indiators of Development". In Rolph Van Ier Hoeven and Richard Anker, ed, *Poverty Monitoring — An International Concern* (New York, St. Martin Press, 1991) pp. 84–94.
23. *Ibid.*
24. See Ravi Kanbur : Poverty and Development in Rolph Van Der Hoeven and Richard Anker, ed., *Poverty Monitoring—An International Concern* (New York, St. Martin Press, 1991), pp. 84–94.
25. See *Human Development Report 1990* (New York, Oxford University Press, 1990).
26. See World Development Report, 1990.

4

DEVELOPMENT INTERVENTIONS

THE SOCIAL STRUCTURE

The principal objective of development is elimination of poverty through a systematic transformation of the village social organisation. Hence any attempt at poverty alleviation without a genuine understanding of social structure is bound to be a failure. Poverty is not merely an economic phenomenon. It is, in fact, a state of social and economic deprivation with deep historical roots.

The Indian society has been basically authoritarian in structure and attitude. The society is hierarchical and each individual has his place in the hierarchy. The authoritarian structure and hierarchical pattern of the society is found within the Indian family. According to Humayun Kabir (Mahine Lectures, 1961), the three major forces of India's misfortune in the past have been authoritarianism, denial of opportunity to all and restriction of knowledge to selected groups.

All these forces are embodied in the caste system and other crucial sectors of village life i.e. land ownership structure. The relationship of castes to the village is harmonious and, often, both are coterminous. In the words of Iravati Karve, the caste has a cell like structure. For subsistence as a caste, it needs certain type of contract and give and take with the people of other castes. A village is the most perfect cell as an area of sustenance, which is self-sufficient, independent and isolated from others through its individuality. In the village, the articulation of one caste to the others is defined and through this is developed an amazing system of self-regulation, which needs no control and supervision, and withstands all interference. The role of individual is well defined in a caste society. He moves within rather the narrow boundaries of behaviour, fixed for the members of the group of which he is a member. Even though great variations of behaviour are allowed in certain aspects of life..., the source of this behavioural variety is this group (caste).

It is, therefore, logical to say that poverty has its location in the caste system. Exclusive reliance on instruments to bring any long-term relief to the poor would prove to be a failure. This is the finding of a cross-national study by Irma Adelman and C.T. Morris. Analysing the social, political and economic indicators from seventy-eight countries, they have concluded that hundreds of millions of people have been hurt rather than helped by economic development.

It is argued by some that poverty is the consequence of development. Poverty is a relative term and is best understood as a product of relations of exchange. Development has given rise to unequal exchange everywhere leading to deprivation of one in relation to the others. Backward village enters into an exchange relation with the outside world through development. To quote Arun Majumdar, agricultural production processes of a developed village drive adjacent villages of petty producers with whom the former enters into exchange relations towards an overall retrogression on the living modes of these villages.[1]

ADULT FRANCHISE AND STRUCTURAL DISEQUILIBRIUM

The introduction of adult franchise has immensely influenced the dynamics of village life. It has also sharpened the conflict among various caste groups as well as between castes and other ethnic groups. There is a marked tendency among numerous strong castes to consolidate themselves for dominance and political authority. The franchise right has enabled the numerically dominant caste to activate the caste organisation and use it for its political gain quite successfully. The caste conflict between the rich minority and the majority 'have-nots' is also in evidence as a result of such mobilisation.

Seen in the background of such conflicts, one finds a trend among many castes to leave the villages and settle in nearby market towns. One also sees the gradual displacement of the traditional leaders who, despite their social authority, fail to compete with the leaders of the poor majority for dominance in the new power structures. However, following the changes in the power structure, there has not been a corresponding change in the motivational patterns and social relationships characterising the village society. This has led to social tension.

Equality of opportunity for all is slowly replacing the restricted access of some caste groups to the avenues of power. Universality of knowledge is being emphasized in place of the monopoly of certain groups over knowledge. These indicate changes in the social dynamics. The real test of the development programmes lies in the contribution they make in developing the competence of village people to function effectively as individuals and in democratic institutions. Development must expedite the process of liquidating what Karve calls the cell of caste while not seriously disturbing the social equilibrium.

DEVELOPMENTAL INTERVENTIONS

The post-Independence era in India has seen a series of development experiments. There have been programmes of sectoral development to develop country's deficient sectors like agriculture as well as programmes of poverty alleviation through integrated rural development. A comprehensive programme called the Community Development Programme has aimed to achieve an all round growth of rural areas. A series of exclusive programmes for the welfare of the Scheduled Castes and the Scheduled Tribes have also been implemented. For the last so many years, co-operatives and the Panchayati Raj Institutions have been playing a key role in the entire process of development by giving it a participatory thrust.

The Food Campaign: The most urgent requirement in the early years of independence was to overcome the acute food scarcity facing the nation. In order to achieve self-sufficiency in foods, the 'Grow More Food' campaign was launched in 1947 and the agriculture sector was accorded topmost priority. The food campaign aimed at assisting the cultivators to increase their production and help them to bring idle lands under cultivation. But the move failed to elicit the desired response from the villagers. The reasons for its failure were many. Firstly, the 'felt' needs of the people such as education, water, health services and, above all, the village conditions were not taken into consideration. Secondly, in India, agriculture was never market-oriented and the people, therefore, did not take risks with the new agricultural practices until they were tested in village conditions. Thirdly, there were no intermediary institutions linking the village with officials. Worse still, the officials had little agricultural knowledge, competence and experience. Fourthly, agriculture as an occupation—specially cultivation by small peasants and agricultural labourers — did not enjoy much social status. Lastly, the role of bureaucracy in implementing agricultural programmes was retrograde. It assumed, often wrongly, superior wisdom in all matters and refused to delegate responsibility to the people.

COMMUNITY DEVELOPMENT PROGRAMME

In early fifties, there was a policy shift from the development of agriculture sector to the composite scheme of community development as a result of the failure of the food experiment. The Narialwala Committee recommended that development must consist of a rural-cum-urban programme involving the building up of a *Growth Centre* nucleus and the development of a rural hinterland. It was to be a composite programme covering all fields of development in the village i.e., agriculture, animal husbandry, fishery, poultry, irrigation, soil conservation, communications, public health, education, social education, rural industrialisation , women's and children's welfare.

The primary task of the community development programme was to develop a *Growth Centre* nucleus from which development would trickle down to surrounding rural areas. To achieve this objective, massive investment was made. This approach was inspired by the success of the Ford Foundation projects on rural development conducted in collaboration with the Government of India.

The Community Development Programme (CDP) had a decision making structure. There was a Central Committee at the national level with the Prime Minister as the Chairman, the members of the Planning Commission and the Minister of Food and Agriculture as its members. There was the Community Projects Administrator (CPA) in charge of planning and directing the programme with the assistance from the concerned ministries.

Extension Services : The National Extension Service was created to meet the public demand for the wide expansion of the programme. It envisaged a nucleus fund. Its staffing pattern was same as in the C.D. Programme. The Block Development Officer acted as the co-ordination officer for 100 villages with a population between 60,000 to 80,000 supported by Extension Officers of various departments. There were ten Village Level Workers, in each Block with a basic a high school level education to be supplemented by some in-service training. New training centres for the BDOs came up along with training centres for women workers, social education organisers and public health workers.

The programme was administered by a Development Commissioner at the State level. Besides, the set up included the Chief Minister as the Chairman of the State Development Committee or Board, with ministers representing departments as members. At the district and Block level, there were committees to ensure implementation of the programme.

The expansion of the programme created difficulties for the Planning Commission which was in charge of the overall supervision. In 1956, a separate Ministry of Community Development was created and the C.D. Programme was taken out of the ambit of the Planning Commission.

ASSESSMENT OF THE C.D. PROGRAMME

Nehru's decision to 'early blanket the country with community development blocks' was based upon the desire to help the villagers to manage their own institutions and solve their problems on a self-help basis. Besides, there were other long range objectives such as development of a country-wide resource base and improvement in the quality of life in village. But these goals were too gigantic to be real. The process of development, as it were, was put on a short circuit. Too much had been attempted in too short a period.

The politicians of the period, especially the members of the Parliament, put pressure on the Nehru Government to expand the programme to their areas. They did it primarily in their own selfish interest. Opening C.D. Block in a particular constituency implied the flow of a lot of new money. Adopting these tactics, politicians made fast bucks, yet later on they hardly missed an opportunity to criticise and condemn the programme.

The Parliament judged the programmes on the basis of

funds committed and targets achieved. Therefore, the technical staff and the administrative personnel were more interested in achieving targets within a prescribed time than in sensitising the people about the need to change and accept change. The bureaucracy treated the programme implementation as a command performance rather than a consensus building effort towards all round village development. The social education approach envisaged in the programme could not be successfully applied because the village society in India was caste-ridden and status-quoist in its orientation.

C.D. PROGRAMME IN THE KANDHAMAL DISTRICT

As part of the expansion of the programme, NES blocks came up in the remote Kandhamal district of Orissa with special schemes for the tribal people. The district (then Phulbani-Boudh) was divided into 15 C.D. blocks covering a population of 602,107. Considerable progress was reported in the field of agriculture, animal husbandry, health and rural sanitation, communication etc. Nine out of 15 C.D. Blocks, including Phulbani Block were declared as Tribal Development Blocks with special emphasis on the tribal welfare.

CONSTITUTIONAL SAFEGUARDS FOR THE TRIBES AND DEVELOPMENT STRATEGIES

The Constitution of India has provisions safeguarding the interests of tribals in the country. The fifth and sixth schedules deal exclusively with the administration of tribal areas. The regions previously known as "excluded areas" have been put under the sixth schedule while those known as "partially excluded" areas and some of the tribal areas in the erstwhile princely states are included in the fifth schedule. It was the responsibility of the Union Government to administer these areas. Its exclusive power extended to giving directions to the state for the good administration of tribal areas and also for the execution of development programmes for tribal communities as a whole. Under the fifth schedule, there is a provision for setting up a Tribal Advisory Council which the Governors may consult while making regulations for tribal development in the scheduled areas. It is an exception to the general norm that the governor does not have to consult the state legislature in the matter related to tribal development. Besides, the state is directed, under the Directive Principles of States Policy, to promote with special care the educational and economic interests of weaker sections of the people in general and the scheduled castes and scheduled tribes in particular. The States are directed to protect the tribals form social injustice and exploitation.

TRIBAL DEVELOPMENT BLOCKS (TDBs)

In 1954, multipurpose Tribal Development Blocks were inaugurated in tribal areas. These blocks were expected to cover all areas of community life of the tribes. But, in course of time, their activities suffered due to budgetary constraints. Like the C.D. Block schemes, the TDB schemes became sectoral programmes aimed at developing agriculture, animal husbandry etc. The tribals living in areas outside the TDBs were deprived of benefits accruing from its programmes except certain educational concessions.

Tribal development became synonymous with the TDB programme. However, they did not take into account the regional variations which affected their implementation adversely. Besides, the criteria followed in the establishment of the Blocks were not free from flaws. As a result of this, only the tribal-majority areas, in which two-thirds of the population were tribals, could have TD Blocks while many deserving tribal groups in several states were deprived of the benefits of similar development programmes. In some places, defective listing of scheduled tribe led to such deprivations. Even in the TD Block areas, it was alleged that benefits did not reach some target groups and basic needs of tribals were not taken into account before extending assistance to them under various development schemes.

The Dhebar Commission (1960–61) pointed out that the constitutional provisions relating to tribal development had not been adequately utilised. It recommended measures for protection of tribal interest in relation to land, forest, excise and marketing. The Shilu Ao Committee complained that the TDB outlays were the only investments for tribals and that no benefit accrued to them from the general schemes of rural development.

TRIBAL AREAS SUB-PLAN (TSP)

In order to overcome the deficiencies of the TDBs in meeting the challenges of tribal development, the Tribal Areas Sub-Plan was introduced. Tribal development came to be viewed as part, that too a special part, of the broad strategy of rural development. It was divided into two segments to ensure faster development of tribals. One segment focussed on the areas of tribal concentrations while the other segment looked after the development of the dispersed tribal population. The first segment addressed itself to the task of meeting the special needs and requirements of tribals. The second segment insisted that tribals used opportunities under general development schemes which are in operation in the region.

It was the responsibility of the state government to administer tribal development under the TSP. The outlays under the plan include a share from the allocations of the State plan, the general sectoral outlays in the state, special central assistance and the institutional finance. The share from the State Plan outlays is determined keeping in view the considerations such as the size of the tribal population, geographical area, level of development and the state of social services. There are provisions under the TSP which guard against any diversion of sub-plan funds to other programmes. The Sub-Plan stipulates exclusive utilisation of funds in the tribal areas. It provides for one unified control over expenditure made through various administrative departments. Besides, there is provision, under the plan, for one-time approval of schemes for the period of the plan as a whole.

At the state level, there is the Development Commissioner for the tribes and a Director of Social Welfare. Below them in the administrative hierarchy, there is a project administrator in the overall charge of implementation of all the plan schemes in the project area. The Collector and the District Development Officers are the key officials supervising the implementation of programmes. There is a District Advisory Council of which the Collector is the Chairman and all district officers of the various departments are members. To assist these officials in the development administration, there is the entire administrative hierarchy of the Panchayat Raj to assist these officials.

PARTICIPATORY DEVELOPMENT

It is necessary to understand the needs of the people whose development the government seeks to promote. This is the first step towards social change. The development ideology should be translated as far as possible into the language and symbols of the people. The village mind should be understood and the development programme explained to the village people in a language which they understand.

At the political level, development requires devolution of power from the centre to the states and from the states to villages. The idea of devolution was expressed clearly in the report of the study team on community development led by Balwantrai Mehta in 1959. The report maintained that the government should divest itself completely of certain duties and responsibilities and entrust them to a body which will have the entire charge of all developmental work within its jurisdiction reserving to itself only the functions of guidance, supervision and higher planning. The team envisaged a three-tier structure of local self-government institutions : the village Panchayat at the base, Panchayat Samiti at the Block level and the Zilla Parishad at the district level.

These institutions provide opportunities for self-expression and political representation at these levels. They also provide opportunities for mobilisation both at the group level and mass level. They have succeeded in getting the central and state governments to respond to village needs. They have also brought about changes in the traditional leadership patterns. In this sense, Panchayati Raj can be described as the incubator for democracy at the grass-root level.

Created through state legislation, the Panchayat Raj Institutions have been integrated into the policy-making apparatus of the country at the local level. In practice, however, they have been acting as social pressure groups through their indulgence in caste and other types of ethnic politics. In spite of this, they have played a positive role in raising the social and political consciousness as well as political participation of villagers. Besides, they have provided a training ground for the political leadership of the future.

In the various areas of rural development, it has helped to create a "participatory thrust" as a concomitant of the general awakening process. In doing so, it has contributed to raising the quality of rural development in terms of the development of human resources. Some concrete benefits have reached the people as a result of the working of the Panchayati Raj. Firstly, the vast army of non-officials in the Community Development and the Panchayati Raj have played an educative role in process of development. Secondly, the concept of local level planning has gained substance through people's participation at each stage. Thirdly, communication channels have opened through the electoral process, making the officials and non-officials respond to people's needs and grievances. Fourthly, programme implementation which was suffering earlier because of the lack of genuine understanding of people's needs has improved in quality with the participation of the local people. The 'empathic' gap has been bridged, as it were, to a great extent.

However, there is a caveat. The general field experience is that at the local level there is an influential minority dominating over the entire population. The minority comprising the rich upper caste people takes part in all the developmental activities while the majority comprising the poor and 'low' caste people have virtually no access to the participation in them. To take an example, digging an irrigation canal would benefit those having large-size land holding who can make use of irrigation facilities rather than the poor agricultural labourers who have no land of their own. Hence, the argument that the local initiatives produce better results in terms of planning and implementation does not always hold good. Even the Planning Commission's Working Group of 1977 under the Chairmanship of M.L. Dantwala, came to the same conclusion after evaluating the programmes.

COOPERATIVES AND TRIBAL DEVELOPMENT IN THE KANDHAMAL DISTRICT

The Cooperative societies, along with Panchayat Raj Institutions, constitute the core of participatory development at the rural level. Their objective is to foster development through people's participation in their organisation and management under the overall supervision of the Department of Cooperation.

The cooperative societies have been created with the specific objective to protect the poor tribals from the clutches of exploitative village landlords and moneylenders. They provide credit facilities to the members with a view to raising their standard of living. Further, they create opportunities for employment especially for the members hailing from agricultural families.

The present Kandhamal district was part of the Boudh-Kandhamal area. The cooperative societies in the area were under the jurisdiction of one Assistant Registrar of Cooperative Societies (A.R.C.S.) of Ganjam district with his office at Berhampur until the creation of a full fledged ARCS circle at Phulbani. The District Registrar of Cooperative Societies of Berhampur Sub-Division was in charge of supervision, of the societies under the Phulbani circle.

In the year 1979, a divisional office was established at Phulbani to cope with the growth in the number of cooperative societies. The area of its jurisdiction was coterminous with the undivided revenue district of Phulbani. There were three cooperative circles in this division, each in-charge of one ARCS, with their headquarters located at the respective Sub-Divisional headquarters.

According to one estimate (1981–82), there are 110 cooperative societies belonging to 15 different categories under the administrative control of Phulbani Division. There has been a steady growth in their membership as well as the volume of the share capital. The total number of members enrolled in these societies as on 1 April 1993 is 1,36,006 as against the total number of 1,49,185 agricultural families, covering 91 per cent of the present population. The scheduled caste and scheduled tribe membership is much higher than that of other castes. Together, the societies have a working capital of Rs. 482.57 lakh (1993–94). The share capital of the societies consists of members subscriptions, and contribution from the government and other corporate bodies.

The cooperative credit structure of the Phulbani Division rests with the Cooperative Central Bank (CCB) with the Head Quarters at Boudh which was part of Phulbani district until

1994. The CCB has six branches in the district: branches at Phulbani, Tikabali, G. Udayagiri, Baliguda, Manamunda and Purunakatak. There are 24 Large Area Multi-purpose Cooperative Societies (LAMPCS) and 40 Service Cooperative Societies at the base of the credit structure and affiliated to the CCB. There are 64 Phulbani Agency Cooperative Societies (PACS) out of which 61 are financed by the CCB. The rest three are LAMPCS in the Kotagarh and Tumudibandh Block which are financed by the State Bank of India.

The Regional Marketing Cooperative Societies (RMCS) located at Boudh and Raikia are engaged in the distribution of agricultural inputs such as fertilizers and pesticides etc.. The lead societies for the public distribution of essential commodities are wholesale cooperative societies at Boudh and Raikia supported by primary cooperative stores and service cooperative societies. Out of 152 Panchayats in the district, 141 Gram Panchayats have been covered by retail outlets.

The Agricultural Marketing Cooperative Society (AMCS) at Tikabali is the most successful cooperative unit in the district. It safeguards the economics interests of the rural tribals by providing reasonable price for minor forest produce procured by them. It also helps in the distribution of different consumer goods through its branches. The society also collects surplus agricultural produce like oil seeds, maize, ragi and other rabi crops for marketing. It maintains a fund out of which needy members are given financial and for education and medical treatment. The society gives royalty to the government for the lease of forest. In course of time, the cooperatives, however, have come under the influence of the local elite leading to a loss of public faith in such organisations.

TRIBAL DEVELOPMENT AND THE ISSUE OF RURAL CREDIT

Development in backward areas has come to be seen primarily as a function of credit. Benefits of development refer to the easy finance made available to the poor through various financial institutions on the recommendations of the development agencies. The purpose of financing the poor is to help them not only to build up an economic base but to create an additional source of income development opportunities for gainful employment.

In the first decade of planning, cooperative credit was provided for the benefit of small farmers in the form of seeds, fertilizers and implements. However, specific needs of various categories of farmers were not taken into consideration. Dominant farmer groups benefited from capital intensive agricultural development under IADP and IAAP.

The Committee of Rural Credit Survey recommended that the government policy must address itself to the cause of small and marginal farmers and also the agricultural labourer. It called for an extensive use of the existing institutional set up rather than creation of new ones.

In principle, the interest of small farmer has always been at the centre of cooperative credit. But, as discovered by the Committee on Cooperative Credit, the cooperative finance was not reaching the small farmers in proportion to their number. The committee directed the primary credit societies to make resources available to the small farmers as far as possible. It insisted on making outright grants to Cooperative Central Banks and Primary Credit Societies. However, its report neglected the long-term credit needs of small farmers while making suggestions for meeting their expedient needs.

The recommendations of the committee were incorporated in the Third Plan. There was a suggestion to make a careful assessment of the extent to which outright grants have led to the extension of credit facilities, In the year 1964, a working group under the Chairmanship of M.V. Mathur was set up to look into the matter.

In 1969, the All India Credit Review Committee under the Chairmanship of B. Venkatappaiah was set up. It not only pointed out the limitations of the government's policy but also made a few recommendations to overcome them. It drew the attention of the government to the controls exercised by the big farmers on the credit institutions. It expressed doubts over the repayment capacity of the small farmers. It suggested liberal borrowing and repayment facilities for them. It made small farmer's membership of cooperative societies mandatory. It recommended the setting up of a Small Farmer's Development Agency to provide financial incentive and security to help them carry out innovations in agriculture. The Fourth Plan incorporated this recommendation of Venkatappaiah Committee.

During the fifth plan, farmer's service societies at Tehsil and Block level were set up to meet the composite needs of the small farmers e.g. credit, supply services, marketing etc. on the recommendations of the National Commission on Agriculture.

BENEFICIARY ATTITUDE TOWARDS CREDIT

Credit issue, like any other issue, is relative in nature. It is related to social and economic status of the beneficiary. While the better-off may use credit for the desired purpose, the poor tend to view it as a windfall and merrily consume it without realising its potential to elevate their economic status. They are very much delimited both in their attitude and capacity to use it for productive purposes. The better off not only can manage to avail themselves of big credit with their sureties of land but also move up in the ladder using the finance. The poor, in consuming the credit, can hope to get temporary relief from the acute pressure of subsistence. Often, the availability of easy credit induces in them a need for more economic assistance and to satisfy this need they resort to unfair and unscrupulous methods. As a result, development which is the purpose of rural credit gets defeated.

We can summaries the implications of rural credit as thus: (a) Rural credit often creates economic divisions in the society because it affects the rich, not-so-rich and the poor very differently. (b)From the beneficiaries' angle, rural credit proves to be a waste.

We may make a few general observations regarding the tribals' attitude to credit in the Kandhamal district. Among the relatively well-off tribals, there is an aversion for taking loans, since it goes against the social norm. Some are reluctant to take loans since they fear that they may not be able to repay which is unethical in their view. Some are afraid of coercive methods of realisation of credit in the event of non-repayment. The poor are the worst affected. Their failure to repay forces them to leave the village. Instead of helping them rehabilitate, it only succeeds in displacing them. This brings us to the issue of selective financing as opposed to indiscriminate and liberal financing. Criticising indiscriminate credit disbursements, often simultaneously by different governmental development agencies in agriculture sector, V.M. Tarkunde observes that the credit institutions constitute a rather imposing superstructure on a deficient and weak base.

DECENTRALISATION OF RURAL CREDIT

In order to streamline the credit planning and decentralise it further, the Reserve Bank of India introduced the Service Area Approach in 1988 with village as the local unit. Under the Service Area Credit Plan, the Commercial Banks, Regional Rural Banks and the Cooperatives were required to draw up their credit plans based on locally exploitable potentials for lending activities and for proper identification of beneficiaries. Village credit plans were to be drawn up on the basis of updated village profiles. Accordingly NABARD embarked on potential-linked-credit plan for five years from 1989–90 to 1994–95 and 1996–97 to co-terminate with the 8th five year plan. Credit estimates related to the potentials which can be exploited for development have been sought to be documented under this plan. The plan has also sought to take into account the changes in priorities of the existing infrastructures to make realistic credit projection.

INTEGRATED TRIBAL DEVELOPMENT PROGRAMME

The ITDA came into existence in 1975 as a part of the Tribal Sub-Plan strategy adopted during the Fifth Five Year Plan. It was envisaged in the Sub-Plan to have ITDP for the integrated development of the areas of tribal concentration. Since the tribal development blocks were too small for implementation of the project programmes, the ITDA was created to meet this purpose under one Project Officer.

The ITDA consists of a governing body for formulating its programmes. There is a Project Officer who executes these programmes. The governing body consists of the District Collector and all heads of developmental departments and the MLAs and the MPs belonging to the district as its members. The Project Officer is the coordinator and the Secretary of the body. Besides the general body, there is a Project Advisory Committee for preparing the plans and reviewing their progress. The Chairman of the Committee is the District Collector.

THE PROJECT OFFICER

The Project Officer is the key official with the overall administrative responsibility of the Agency. There is no fixed tenure for him. His continuance as the Project Officer depends on the discretion of the government. Yet, a term of at least 2 to 3 years is generally favoured to enable him to understand the complexities of administration in the tribal areas and contribute for the development of these areas.

The functions discharged by the Project Officer are of a routine nature. He is responsible for executing the policies and programmes formulated by the Governing Body. The following are the functions of the Project Officer, as envisaged in the sub-plan strategy:

(*a*) Identification and demarcation of areas of tribal concentration.

(*b*) Identification of primitive pockets for special attention for development under the package programme.

(*c*) Recognition of more backward communities.

(*d*) Formulation of tribal sub-plan and preparation of Integrated Tribal Development Project report.

(*e*) Coordination between local development officers and the higher authorities.

(*f*) According of financial sanctions for schemes within his powers.

(*g*) Coordination and supervision of all developmental activities in the sub-plan areas.

(*h*) Preparation of periodic progress reports of schemes.

(*i*) Implementation of protective legislations.

(*j*) Acting as the Member-Secretary of the Advisory Committees on Tribal Development.

Although the Project Officer has been entrusted with so much of responsibility, he lacks necessary powers to effectively discharge them. Firstly, he does not have power to control the staff working under him. Similarly, he does not have any control over the Block Development Officers and other staff of the Tribal Development Blocks who are directly responsible for the implementation of ITDA programmes. Further, he has no power of inspection although he is required to coordinate and review the progress of different schemes implemented in the project area. In the matter of finance, his power is limited to the sanction of schemes to the tune of Rs. 1000 only.

However, in the year 1987, the government made ITDA a single line agency in the sub-plan area for the speedy development of the tribal areas and introduced several measures to strengthen the position of the Project Officer. The measures are as follows:

(*a*) Elevation of the cadre of the Project Officer to that of Sub-Collector and Additional District Magistrate.

(*b*) Vesting in the Project Officer the powers of inspection, review and reporting on all officers and institutions operating in the Project area.

(*c*) Appointments to the posts in the Sub-Plan area by a selection committee with the Project Officer as its Chairman.

(*d*) Making all the officers of various department in charge of the programmes of the ITDA responsible to the Project Officer.

However, these additional measures did not bring about any significant change in the authority and position of the Project Officer. In spite of the government's attempt to evolve a single line administration in the tribal areas, there is overlapping and duplication in the administrative framework of tribal development.

The programmes implemented by the ITDA can be classified in to seven categories:

1. Agricultural and Allied Programmes
2. Educational Programmes
3. Industrial Development Programmes
4. Health Programmes
5. Electrification Programmes

6. Irrigation Development Programmes
7. Special Schemes.

The strategy of ITDA for developing tribal agriculture has the following objectives:

1. Maximisation of the yield from land by supplying necessary inputs and providing infrastructural facilities in order to raise their living standards.
2. Dissemination of knowledge of modern and improved practices to the tribal farmers.
3. Weaning away the tribals from the practice of shifting cultivation.
4. Transformation of subsistence agriculture into market-oriented agriculture.

The development of animal husbandry in tribal areas is as important as agricultural development. The ITDA has taken up several animal husbandry and livestock improvement programmes. These include distribution of milch and drought animals to the tribals on subsidy basis, starting of livestock farms to produce good breeding for upgrading the quality of the cattle and establishment of the milk chilling centres to facilitate the marketing of the milk produced by the tribals. In addition to these, there are provisions for starting of veterinary institutions to treat the diseases of the cattle, supply of goat and sheep units and poultry units to tribals on subsidy basis.

In the field of health, the ITDA aims at strengthening the existing medical institutions like Primary Health Centres and other types of hospitals and opening of new medical centres where there is no such centre. Besides, it has plans for eradication of communicable diseases and intensification of family planning programmes.

The ITDAs have also taken up the job of spreading education in tribal areas on a priority basis because the rate of literacy here is very low compared to the plain areas. They aim at opening primary schools in bigger villages and residential Ashram Schools in clusters of sparsely populated villages. They also seek to equip the tribal children properly with books, writing materials, dresses and other incentives.

Under the ITDP, there are minor irrigation programmes, industrial programmes and electrification programmes in the general category.

SPECIAL PROGRAMMES UNDER THE ITDP

ITDP has taken steps to uplift the tribal groups, like *Kandhas, Gadabas and Parajas.* These communities have been picked up for special treatment on the basis of their socio-cultural and economic backwardness. The families belonging to these tribal groups are assisted under the ITDP with the supply of necessary inputs to enable them to cross the poverty line. Since these tribal groups practice shifting cultivation they are not only provided with lands, they are also assured of help with regard to land development and soil conservation. They are supplied inputs like plough bullocks, HYV seeds, fertilisers, persticides etc. on 100 per cent subsidy basis. Under the ITDP, they are also assured of a second source of income to supplement the income from agriculture through provision for sheep and goat units, poultry units and bee-keeping boxes for extraction of honey.

ITDP launched a special scheme in 1984 to rehabilitate the *podu* cultivators. The practice of *podu* cultivation resulted in loss of forest cover which in turn led to soil erosion, loss of fertile soil and disturbance of the ecological balance. The scheme known as Economic Rehabilitation of *podu* cultivators aims at diverting the tribals from this harmful practice. Its objectives are:

1. Rehabilitation on degraded hill slopes through social conservation and social forestry.
2. Rehabilitation through development of wasteland

and supply of necessary inputs like seeds, fertilizers, bullocks.

3. Developments of orchards and other fruit plantations on degraded hill slopes along with inter-cropping with suitable dry crops.
4. Providing financial assistance to the tribals on subsidy basis to start small scale industries like stone crushing, basket making, bee-keeping, backyard poultry etc.
5. Providing irrigation facilities for the lands allotted to the tribals.
6. Taking up the plantation of medicinal plants in the lands allotted to the tribals.

There is, no doubt, that the schemes under ITDP were quite ambitious. However, studies have revealed a number of flaws in the working of ITDAs. The flaws include administrative weaknesses, incongruities in financial management, absence of any provision for people's participation in the designing and implementation of the programmes, absence of an active monitoring and evaluation mechanism etc. Timely allocation of funds has been the single-most important problem. As M. Bapuji remarks "Rather than ITDA getting finances every year to match its programmes, it has to tailor its plans and programmes to the funds it received from various sources".[2] A result of this, the ITDA is not in a position to project an integrated thrust of various sectors.

INTEGRATED TRIBAL DEVELOPMENT PROGRAMME IN THE KANDHAMAL DISTRICT

ITDP is a comprehensive development package for tribals in select areas having tribal concentrations. Under the programme, special schemes for tribals have been introduced to be administered by the Integrated Tribal Development

Agencies operating in the district. The Kandhamal District has three ITDAs working for the uplift of the *Kandhas* at the three Sub-Divisions of Phulbani, G. Udyagiri and Baliguda.

The programme aims at infrastructure development, poverty amelioration and educational programmes. There is a Project Level Committee (PLC) of the ITDA which prepares the action plan. The members of the PLC are the concerned MLAs, MPs, the BDOs and the official representatives from different departments of the government. The Block Office has the responsibilities of implementing the programmes with the help of various departments of the government at the district level.

Table 4.1
Physical Achievement of ITDA, Phulbani[3]

Year	*Target*	*Number of Beneficiaries Assisted*
1980–81	Nil	06
1981–82	Nil	52
1982–83	Nil	86
1983–84	250	116
1984–85	250	222
1985–86	115	80
1986–87	42	59
1987–88	150	136
1988–89	200	321
1989–90	200	214
1990–91	200	213
1991–92	200	214

The ITDA of Phulbani is actively involved in the development of the tribals assisting them through various income generating schemes. According to the official sources, its performance has been remarkable, its achievement often surpassing the targets. The table above shows the number of beneficiaries assisted between 1980–81 and 1991–92.

INTEGRATED RURAL DEVELOPMENT PROGRAMME (IRDP)

IRDP is the most massive rural development intervention since independence. Its primary objective is to reduce rural poverty through infrastructural development. The administrative machinery and the agencies entrusted with the implementation of the programme have recorded exemplary performance as far as target achievement is concerned. The pace of development has been quite rapid in the 1980s and after.

Under the programme selected families are given financial assistance to cross the poverty line through the strategy of productive assets endowment. The income level of the beneficiaries is sought to be raised, on a lasting basis for which the factors of local resources, infrastructural support, and market linkages available to the beneficiaries are taken into account.

The target group comprises beneficiary families of small farmers, marginal farmers, labourers, non-agricultural labourers and artisans whose family income is below Rs. 11,000 per annum. The financial assistance consists of subsidy and bank loan. The extent of subsidy is 25 per cent for the small farmers, 33.3 per cent for marginal farmers, agricultural labourers and artisans and 50 per cent for tribal families. The individual family may receive subsidy to the tune of Rs. 3,000 in normal areas, Rs. 4,000 in DPAP areas and Rs. 5,000 for tribal families. It is stipulated that 50 per cent of the assisted families should belong to the scheduled castes and scheduled tribes.

SCHEMES UNDER IRDP

IRDP has schemes in the primary, secondary and tertiary sectors. In the primary sector, there are schemes for minor irrigation works and schemes for the supply of milch animals, poultry, sheep, goats, ducks, plough bullocks etc. Families are also assisted to avail themselves of schemes like pottery, carpentry, repair and maintenance works, shops, leather works, supply of bullock carts, rickshaws etc.

While the Central and State governments provide finance and lay down the broad guidelines for its planning and implementation, the main administrative unit for its implementation is the District Rural Development Agency, with the Collector at the helm of its affairs. However, the most crucial level in the implementation is the block which is the basic unit for the preparation of perspective and annual plans. The block ensures the implementation of the programme as per the approved plan. It also provides feed back on the impact of the programme.

BENEFICIARY IDENTIFICATION

Identification of beneficiaries forms an integral part of planning under the IRDP. It is done according to a specific criterion and in several stages. The stages include household survey, preparation of the initial list of beneficiaries, rectification of the list by the Panchayat Samiti and finally approved by the DRDA. The list of beneficiaries is then published and circulated for the knowledge of concerned departments, agencies and the people.

ANNUAL ACTION FLAN

At the time of implementation, the District Plan is sent by the DRDA to the various sectoral heads in the district who decide the annual action plan and the resource allocation. The annual action plan is then sent to the block for execution. Programmes are distributed scheme-wise and financial institutions are entrusted with the job of processing the credit to be extended to the selected beneficiaries.

COMMITTEE HIERARCHY FOR CREDIT PLANNING

There is a hierarchy of committees to tackle the credit issue. At the national level, there is a high level committee on credit support under the Chairmanship of the Secretary, Department of Rural Development. The committee consists of representatives form the RBI, the NABARD, the commercial banks, the State Governments, the Planning Commission, Banking and Insurance Division of Ministry of Finance and Ministry of Industry. This committee reviews credit arrangements and recommends changes and improvements. The State Level Coordination Committee is there to guide DRDAs in planning, implementation and monitoring. It seeks to ensure departmental coordination and linkages for the programme. There is the District Consultative Committee at the district level. The Consultative Committee at the Block level coordinates the activities of the Bank and Block officials. There is also a Beneficiaries' Advisory Committee at the block level. There are sub-committees at the Panchayat level. Every year, 600 families below the poverty line are identified for assistance in each block. Credit camps and Credit Recovery Camps are conducted at the block level for effective documentation of credit utilisation.

PERFORMANCE OF THE DRDA IN THE KANDHAMAL DISTRICT

In the Kandhamal district, the performance of the DRDA during the 6th and 7th Plans in achieving its targets has been claimed to be above expectations . During the 6th plan, it covered 39,955 families out of which 25,916 families belonged to the scheduled castes and scheduled tribes. Out of the total investment of Rs. 954.97 lakhs, credit mobilisation was to the tune of Rs. 602.54 lakhs and subsidy utilisation was worth Rs. 352.43 lakhs.

During the 7th plan, 47,438 families were assisted out of which 31,257 belonged to the scheduled castes and scheduled tribes. The total amount invested for the district under the programme was Rs. 11038.32 lakhs out of which credit mobilisation was of the order of Rs. 675.43 lakhs and subsidy, Rs. 432.89 lakhs.

PERFORMANCE OF IRDP IN THE PHULBANI BLOCK

In the decade between 1980–81 to 1989–90, 3018 households have benefited against a target of 4,570 in the Phulbani block alone. Out of them, 486 beneficiaries have also been covered under the Second Dose Scheme. Under the multiple (basket) scheme, 361 beneficiaries were covered in the 1980s. According to one estimate, out of the families covered under the IRDP, nearly 8 per cent (234 households) crossed the poverty line during the period.

THE MACHINERY OF IMPLEMENTATION: THE BDO

Within tile official hierarchy of the district, the Block Development Officer occupies the most important position as far as implementation of developmental programmes are concerned. Through the BDOs, the district development agencies, the financial institutions, the concerned departments of government, the Block level officials and the village functionaries are brought to a common meeting point. The A to Z of implementation of various programmes of rural and tribal development is carried out under the strict supervision of the BDO. He is consulted by the government departments such as Soil Conversation, Forestry, Irrigation etc. for the data regarding feasibility of the programmes. The BDO is assisted by one Additional Block Development Officer posted in the Block and an army of 15 extension officers drawn from various departments of the government who act as the field staff of the Block. From among the Extension Officers, one is posted as the Progress Assistant who is the core functionary of the Block in the matters of development. He keeps all statistics and records regarding the basic information of the area and also the developmental taken up there. The details of the activities of Extension Officers is given in the form of a table (See Table 4.2).

VILLAGE LEVEL WORKER AS THE DEVELOPMENT COMMUNICATOR

The institution of the village level workers has become indispensable to all developmental activities in the village and thus it has come to occupy a special place in the development literature. They have served as the channels of communication between the block and the village. They have been educating the villagers about the programmes and their usefulness for them. Through them, access of the villagers to the development agencies and financial institutions is facilitated.

Right from the community development days, they have been instrumental in creating the climate within the villages for the technical ministries to serve the needs of the people related to agriculture, family planning, sanitation, drinking water, housing, irrigation, communication etc.. Departments of government often used them as an extension of the bureaucratic arm. In addition to this, the VLWs sometimes are assigned such uncomfortable task as collecting 'small savings' from the people, pressing people to repay loans, supervising the distribution of rations etc.

The burdens of the VLW have increased with the expansion of developmental schemes. He operates at multiple levels as part of the programme imperative. Under the IRDP, his job is manifold. He makes a household survey in the villages to identify the families to be assisted. Then he selects suitable activities for the families, based on his first hand knowledge of village conditions. He motivates and mobilises.

Table 4.2
List of Extension Officers and Their Duties

Sl. No	*The Extension Officers*	*Core Departments*	*Their Duties*
1.	Welfare Extension Officer (WEO)	Harijan and Tribal Welfare	i. Rehabilititation of bonded labourers. ii. Prevent exploitation of scheduled castes and scheduled tribes. iii. Distribution of pre-matric scholarships and text books to scheduled castes and scheduled tribes. iv. Management of Primary School Hostels.
2	Additional Welfare Extention Officer (AWEO)	Harijan and Tribal Welfare	-do-
3.	Cooperative Extension Officer (CEO)	Cooperative Department	i. To organise cooperative policies. ii. Acts as the arbitration authority relating to loan recovery. iii. Acts as the liquidator of societies. iv. Supervises agricultural development works.
4.	Additional CEO	Cooperative Department	-do-
5.	Fishery Extension Officer (FEO)	Fishery Department	Development of pisciculture in the Block.

6.	Sericulture Extension Officer (SEO)	Sericulture Department	Development of sericulture in the Block.
7.	Industrial Promotion Officer (IPO)	Industry Department	i. Development of handicrafts/small scale ii. industries. In-charge of ERRP.
8.	Social Education Officer (SEO)	Youth and Welfare Department	i. Organising Yuvak Sangh and Manila Samiti. ii. Feeding schemes. iii. Social welfare programmes.
9.	Gram Panchayat Extension Officer	Rural Development Department	i. Supervision of the Gram Panchayats. ii. Credit meetings of Panchayat Samitis. iii. Maintenance of records, preparation of reports.
10.	Sub Inspector (Schools I)	Education Department	i. Inspection of schools. ii. Orientation of teachers.
11.	Sub Inspector (Schools II)	-do-	-do-
12.	Junior Engineer (I)	Public Works Department	Give estimate, inspect execution construction work such as road, buildings, dug wells, houses etc.
13.	Junior Engineer (II)	Irrigation Department	Give estimate and plan, inspect execution of irrigation projects.
14.	Marketing Inspector	Civil Supplies Department	i. In charge of fair price shops. ii. Supply of ration to people.

He guides them to take right kind of loans and utilise them properly. Through him, new ideas are communicated to the villager and resources of the government are mobilised to the village. To the illiterate and the gullible villages, he is the proverbial friend, philosopher and the guide. The adopting Extension Officers including the Progress Assistant monitor his activities during execution of development schemes.

Given the diversity of functions of the VLWs, the government must provide them with better incentives and elevate their status commensurate with their work. It must provide adequate in-service training back-up to them. It must ensure a strong supervision of their work. All this, it is hoped, will go a long way to enhance his commitment to the people and indirectly, help reduce dependence of villagers on grass-root politicians.

ANCILLARIES OF THE IRDP

TRYSEM (Training of Rural Youth for Self-Employment Scheme) is a major ancillary of the IRDP intended to impart training to the poor beneficiaries so as to make them capable of maintaining and utilizing their assets and to generate income through self–employment ventures. The physical achievement under this scheme has been much ahead of its target. In 1991–92, the target was to cover 4309 families while the actual number of beneficiaries was 5085. Again in 1992–93, the scheme was to cover 3591 families but it actually covered 4110 families. In 1991–92 a total of Rs. 1,59,32,000 was spent while the expenditure in 1992–93 was Rs. 1,32,76,000.

DWACRA (Development of Women and Children in Rural Areas) is the other major ancillary of the IRDP. It aims at providing opportunities of self–employment to women members of rural families living below the poverty line. The scheme was introduced in 1992–93. The scheme is applicable to groups of women rather than individual women. Each

DWACRA group consists of 10 to 15 members for taking up economic activities suitable to their skill, aptitude and local conditions. In 1992–93, the target was to cover 50 groups and the achievement was one hundred per cent. The total outlay for the year was 7.60 lakhs and the expenditure was 4.10 lakhs.

EMPLOYMENT SCHEMES

The major employment schemes which have been operating in the district are National Rural Employment Programme (NREP) and the Rural Labour Employment Guarantee Programme (RLEGP) and Jawahar Rojgar Yojana (JRY) after the merger of the two in 1989.

Under the NREP, 334 assets were created and 3,25,281 mandays generated between 1980–81 to 1989–90. There was also the (RLEGP) under which 14 school buildings were built and 58,533 mandays were created between 1984–85 to 1989–90.

The JRY aimed at providing gainful employment to the rural poor through creation of durable assets like Indira Awas houses, tree plantations, improvement of rural roads, land reclamation, removal of rural tanks, construction of primary school buildings, excavation of million wells for the purpose of irrigation etc. This scheme provides individual benefit to scheduled caste and scheduled tribe and free bonded labourers. During the year 1991–92 and 1992–93 the achievement under the JRY was quite good. With the assistance from the scheme, 16.2 lakh mandays were created in 1991–92 while, in 1992–93 the achievement exceeded the target by two lakhs.

During five years between 1984–85 to 1989–90, 76 Indira Awas Yojana were constructed. Under the Employment and Rural Rehabilitation Programme, 1354 beneficiaries were covered against a target of 1830.

DROUGHT PRONE AREA PROGRAMME (DPAP)

The Drought Prone Area Programme (DPAP) was introduced in the district in 1975 to mitigate the drought situation covered due to uneven distribution of rainfall and long dry spells. Some of the important components of the programme are (i) development and management of water resources (ii) soil and water conservation measures (iii) afforestation and development of pasture lands (iv) livesotck development etc. The project covered all the 14 blocks of the Kandhamal district.

PROBLEMS FACING IMPLEMENTATION

The implementation of development programmes has exposed serious lapses everywhere. Firstly, the beneficiaries' access to information about various development programmes and agencies of development administering these programmes is reported to be very little. As a result, there is an excessive dependence on the already overworked village level workers for information. The financial aspects of the programme are not properly communicated to the villagers. For example, direct transfer of the subsidy part of the credit from the Small Farmers' Development Agency to the Funding Agency intended to ensure its proper utilisation was not known to the small farmers on the state of Karnataka. This had badly affected their enthusiasm to avail the subsidy.

Big landowners connived with revenue officials to show false land data. This practice has developed in order to evade the land ceiling laws. Moreover, the land records available with the offices are hardly foolproof.

There is a noticeable lag between what the programmes aim to achieve and what the people actually need. According to the area approach, the schemes are chosen on the basis of the resource position and potentials in the area. In practice, however, there is no evidence of systematic management planning prior to implementation of schemes.

It is revealed from some studies that in spite of security and other financial incentives, the small farmers have not availed many schemes, requiring high investment because of their appalling economic conditions and also because of their extremely low replaying capacity.

Preference for various schemes is rarely guided by long-term productivity orientation. It is guided rather by their immediate needs such as rise in income, water shortage, easy repayment facility etc. The needs of small farmers have not been listed according to their priorities over a certain span of time. Besides, there has not been any serious attempt to link the execution of the programme with its outcome in the subsequent stages.

Financial institutions are generally reluctant to provide credit to small farmers. The reasons are attributed to absence of adequate assets, their low repayment capacity and inadequate social and political contacts.

There are procedural constraints for availing loans. Even when loans are sanctioned it takes a lot of time to disburse those because of procedural hassels. As a result, the farmers have turned to the professional money lenders who charge exorbitant rates of interest.

Although there are a number of funding agencies, there is a marked preference for some over others. Some prefer cooperative societies for low rates of interest and for their proximity to the beneficiaries' place of residence. Others prefer banks for correct maintenance of accounts and for quick service. Some others prefer private money lenders because of their accessibility and quick service. There is a overall lack of fit between the organisation and the environment which is a fundamental cause of failure of development programmes.

ASSESSING THE IMPLEMENTATION OF DEVELOPMENT PROGRAMMES—A LITERATURE SURVEY

Having gone through the various development plans and their performance at a general level and particularly in the Kandhamal District, a brief assessment of their implementation may be in order to identify the gaps between planning and practice. For this purpose, we have picked up specific areas such as identification of beneficiaries, selection of schemes, sectoral allocations, ultlisation of loans and assets, growing indebtedness and poor tribal's access to loan etc.

The implementation of a development programme starts with the identification of the target group or the beneficiaries. The criterion currently adopted for such identification is community consensus. The norm for the VLW is to select them in public meetings. Studies have shown that the VLW is usually under the influence of local political leaders both within and outside the Panchayat. Hence beneficiaries picked up by him happen to be their supporters.[4] Consequently, the choice is rarely restricted to families with holdings of 5 acres and less. Some beneficiaries even own 10 to 20 acres of land, while a large number of non-beneficiaries who are in the category of 1 to 5 acres of landholdings are left out of the scheme. Some studies indicate that the non-beneficiary group constitules about 50 per cent of the landless households.[5] Hence we may say that the method of identification adopted benefits largely the landowning families of the upper bracket and leaves out of its ambit the landless poor who constitute the rural majority.

As for selection of schemes for the beneficiaries go, serious lapses have been observed. Relevant studies have revealed a few things in this regard:

(*a*) The beneficiaries are hardly aware of the sources of borrowing.

(*b*) The schemes are generally thrust on the beneficiaries without any prior thinking as to whether the schemes are beneficial to them or not.

(*c*) There is a lack of effective organisation for creating awareness among rural poor about such schemes. As a result, the poorest of the poor who need them the most hardly avail such benefits. Their miserable socio-economic condition can be attributed to this lack of awareness.[6]

(*d*) Although the sixth plan stipulated that two-thirds of the schemes should be in the primary sector and one-third in industry, business and service, sectoral allocations have been made in violation of the above norm. In practice, the whole programme has been reduced to the distribution of bullocks and buffaloes—this over emphasis on animal husbandry is obviously due to the fact that it renders target fulfilment easier and also provides ample scope for leakages and abuses.[7]

UTILISATION OF LOANS AND ASSETS

Under the IRDP schemes, the beneficiaries are provided bullocks for the purposes of cultivation. In reality, as some studies reveal instead of giving a pair of them at one time, only one is given and the other one is supplied after a lapse of a year or two. In some villages bullocks are supplied much before the starting of one ploughing season. In some others they are supplied after the agricultural operations are virtually complete. In some cases bullocks are too young or too old to be of any use.[8] Further, there are manipulations in the purchase of bullocks and other assets owing to the hold the middlemen have over the purchase.

The supply of fertilizers and pesticides for the purpose of cultivation is very common. Since the tribals are traditional users of cow dung manure they cannot accept the supply of fertilizers etc. without some kind of malice. Given the reluctance of the tribals to use such supplies, the non-tribals virtually snatch these inputs from them at very low rates of interest.[9]

Planning Commission has found fault with the administrative structure for this state of affairs. The delivery system, according to the Commission has not been effective in tribal areas because there have been inadequacies in the administrative machinery, lack of sensitive and trained management, lack of general preparedness for large investment, deficiency in accounting systems, procedural delays and lack of proper monitoring and evaluation.

According to some studies, cooperative credit also has been misused. LAMPCS have been extending credit for production purposes such as land development, dug wells purchase of fertilizers and pesticides, sheds, goats, bullocks, sheep, pigs. But actually loan amount has been utilised for non-productive purposes.[10&11]

In Orissa's Kandhamal district, it has been pointed out that 30.6 per cent of *Kandha* beneficiaries are continuing with the schemes and maintaining their assets.[12] The findings of study of the IRDP implementation in the Ananthpur district of Andhra Pradesh show that majority of scheduled castes and tribes are agricultural labourers, non-agricultural labourers and rural artisans. Under the IRDP, assets have been supplied in both the groups. In case of the scheduled castes beneficiaries, only 30.82 per cent have retained the given assets and properly utilised them and 69.18 per cent have sold their assets. In case of scheduled tribes, 53.75 per cent have retained their assets and 46.25 per cent have sold their assets. Among the scheduled caste beneficiaries, only 14.34 per cent have crossed the poverty line, while the percentage of scheduled tribe beneficiaries to have crossed the poverty line is 31.50 per cent. Among the other castes beneficiaries, 24.66 per cent have crossed the poverty line. The investigator had collected, the primary data in all these cases from the field survey. The beneficiaries selected had been provided assets during 1989 and 1992.[13]

RISING INCIDENCE OF INDEBTEDNESS

Some of the programmes were aimed at alleviating the indebtedness of the tribals to the private moneylenders. According to some studies, the contribution of credit and multi-purpose co-operative societies towards this end has not at all been significant.[14&15] This fact is further emphasized in some other studies which have pointed out that the non-institutional sector constitute an important credit agency as in the states of Meghalaya, Assam and Manipur (Gaitonde 1982; 36). These studies further reveal that two-third of the tribals had borrowed at interest rates of 25 per cent per annum or more (Sambrani and Pichholiaya 1975; 69). The tribal faces the market not with marketable surplus but largely with commodities for distress sale to repudiate his debt. In the free market, he is exploited by the merchants and moneylenders not only as buyers but also on sellers.[16]

Under the IRDP, as soon as a beneficiary is identified and loan and subsidy disbursed, he is presumed to have crossed the poverty line. This is a grossly misleading assumption. In reality, the so-called productive assets fail to generate incremental income required to repudiate debts within the stipulated period of time. The volume of indebtedness has increased tremendously over a period of time. The beneficiaries are not only indebted to the banks with compound interest liability of 10 per cent but they have also become indebted to moneylenders who charge 50 per cent rate of interest. Ironically enough, the majority of the beneficiaries had a zero level of indebtedness before receiving help from the various development schemes. Thus, instead of crossing the poverty line, the beneficiaries have been pushed down further owing to the post-scheme debt-burden.[17]

SHRINKING ACCESS OF TRIBALS TO LOANS

From the above discussion, it becomes clear that, compared to other communities, the practical access of tribals to loans is gradually shrinking. The reasons for this are partly endogenous and partly exogenous. The endogenous reason is tribal community's attitude towards credit, infrastructural inputs in agriculture and towards land. The exogenous reasons are lack of proper motivation to change this attitude as well as lack of proper information about benefits.

Modernization of agriculture which is at the heart of the entire development process is the main challenge to the traditional way of tribal life. Productivity is emphasized in the place of consumption. This has far reaching implications, because producing for market denotes a change towards commercialisation of agriculture. Producing more in a small patch of land is preferred to possessing more land and producing little. Under the pretext of commercialisation, a lot of tribal land has been transferred from tribals to non-tribals. Such transfers have resulted in the loss of tribal community's control over its land resources. This transfer of land is effected in many ways. Under conditions of tribal indebtedness, the land belonging to the tribals is mortgaged. Often it is done through an oral exchange. In times of acute poverty, tribals are advised by the more intelligent non-tribals to conceal their identity and give away their lands, violating the rule regarding the non-transfer of tribal land. Another means of land alienation is fictitious adoption and marriage without any legal evidence. In some cases tribal land is hired for some years and finally taken possession of by the non-tribals.

A study of land alienation in the state of Tamil Nadu (Rao and Bhaskardoss 1987; 154) reveals that 57 per cent of the tribals have parted with their lands to meet the consumption expenditure while 20 per cent of them have given away their lands to repay the debts. The study also reveals that, on an average, there is a loss of 1.38 acres per every tribal household and 3.68 acres per every affected household due to alienation of tribal lands.

The use of land records is rarely seen among tribals. Further there is no serious attempt to make these records available to them and educate them about their use. In the absence of such statutory records (Record of Right etc.) the commercial banks and other financial institutions generally refuse to provide long-term loans to tribals[18]. This has resulted in the tribal deprivation in getting any substantial financial help.

Because of the reasons already cited, and because of lack of land owners' exact idea as to his possessions, a correct assessment of the tribal landholdings has become an extremely different job. To assess the poverty line on the basis of landholding therefore becomes all the more misleading. This has led to manipulation of the landholding limits to suit the poverty line criterion. Since the productivity of land in tribal areas is miserably low, the size of the landholding is manipulated (increased) substantially to facilitate finance to the tribals.

Moreover, poverty line cannot be viewed as a static thing. Measured in monetary terms, it must provide for the inflation factor.[19] Unit the Sixth Five Year Plan, this dynamic aspect of poverty line was ignored in the identification of programme beneficiaries as well as on the question of assistance. The income level therefore remained static. The poverty line remained stationary at Rs. 3500 up to 1984-85. Although the claims were made that the poorest had benefited, a larger number of them remained outside the purview of these schemes.

REFERENCES

1. See Arun Majumdar, *Poverty, Development and Exchange Relations — A Study of two Birbhum Villages* (New Delhi, Radiant, 1987).
2. See M. Bapuji, *Tribal Development Administration* (Delhi, Kanishka Publishing House, 1993).
3. Source: Integrated Tribal Development Agency, Phulbani.
4. See K. Sundaram and Suresh V. Tendulkar "Integrated Rural Development Programme in India", *Social Action* (New Delhi) Vol. 35, January–March 1985, pp. 1–25.
5. See H. Pais and C.S.K. Singh, "Rural Development Policies and Inequalities", *Social Action* (New Delhi), January–March 1987, pp. 28–44.
6. See AV. Rama Rao, *Evaluation of Integrated Tribal Development Agency, Khammam District, Andhra Pradesh.* (Hyderabad, the Indian Institute of Economics, 1982).
7. See R.N. Tripathy *et al.*, "Tribal Development Programmes in Keonjhar, Orissa — An Evaluation", N1RD (Hyderabad), 1979.
8. *Ibid.*
9. *Ibid.*
10. See Ranjit Gupta, ed., *Planning for Tribal Development* (New Delhi, Ankur Publishing House, 1976).
11. See A.V. Rama Rao, *Evaluation of Integrated Tribal Development Agency, Khammam District, Andhra Pradesh.* (Hyderabad, the Indian Institute of Economics, 1982).
12. See S.K. Choudhary , "Tribal Development: Dimensions of Planning and Implementation", *Indian Anthropologist* (New Delhi) June-December 1990, pp. 49–66.
13. See M. Jayaraju, "IRDP in Eliminating Poverty Among the Scheduled Castes and Scheduled Tribes", *Economic Affairs,* 38(2), April–June 1993, pp. 111–13.
14. See A.V. Rama Rao, *Evaluation of Integrated Tribal Development Agency, Khammam District, Andhra Pradesh.* (Hyderabad, the Indian Institute of Economics, 1982),
15. See Tribal Culture Research and Training Institute, *Evaluation Study Report on Tribal Development Programmes of ITDA Palmancha Khammam District* (Hyderabad, Tribal Welfare Department: Andhara Pradesh, 1986).

16. See H. Pais and C.S.K. Singh, "Rural Development Policies and Inequalities", *Social Action* (New Delhi), January–March 1987, pp. 28–44.
17. See N.V.M. Rao and P. Raman Reddy "Minor Irrigation and Tribal Development : An Empirical Study" Kurukshetra Vol. 34, No. 2, 1985, pp. 31–33.
18. See B.K. Roy Burman, *Towards poverty Alleviation Programmes in Nagaland and Manipur* (Delhi, Mittal Publications, 1984).
19. See K. John Mammen, "Perceptions of Poverty", *Indian Express* (New Delhi), March 4, 1988.

5

THE PROCESS OF DEVELOPMENT

In the foregoing chapter, we have discussed at length the implementation of development programmes in the Khandhamal district of Orissa and its impact on the people. In this chapter, we propose to focus on the development process and its impact on the people of one particular Gram Panchayat selected for the present study, namely the Alami Gram Panchayat.

THE GRAM PANCHAYAT: A PROFILE

The Alami Gram Panchayat is a relatively new entity coming under the Phulbani Block. It did not feature in the original list of 10 G.Ps coming under the block. It was bifurcated from Tudipaju Gram Panchayat on Dec., 13, 1991 and added to the list, raising the number of GPs under the block to 11. The block is in the heart of the district and the GP is in the heart of the block. The villages of the GP are not concentrated in one area. They are situated on both sides of the Phulbani town. Some are situated close to the township while others are at a considerable distance.

There are, in all, 15 villages under Alami GP out of which one Khajuribida is uninhabited. The inhabited ones are: Teraguda, Nedipada, Pitabari, Bandhasihi, Lengersahi, Mula Rujangi, Bulungi, Alami, Nuaripadar. Majaganda, Sarupada, Sainipadar, Satanjargi and Luhurubali. These villages can be broadly divided into four broad types: (1) Exclusively Tribal (2) Tribal Dominated (3) Exclusive Scheduled Caste Village (4) Scheduled Caste Dominated. The exclusive tribal villages are Pitabari, Sarupada, Satanjargi, Bulungi, Majaganda, Mula Rujangi and Nuaripadar. The villages with a tribal majority are Bandhasahi, Lengersahi, Alami and Teraguda. There is one exclusive scheduled caste village, namely; Sainipadar, while Luhurubali and Nedisahi are two villages in which the *Pana* caste dominates.

The G.P. has a total population of 2413 out of which 1571 are tribals belonging to the Kandha Tribe, 732 are from the *Pana* caste, a lower stratum of the Hindu caste hierarchy and 110 belong to other castes. The total number of households in the GP is 604. Some of the villages have direct contact with the plains since these are located in the outskirts of the town while others are far away from it. For example, Teraguda, Nedisahi and Lengersahi and Bandhasahi are located at the college end of the town by the sides of the state highway No. 7 (Phulbani to Durgaprasad) which is also the main road running through the town one will come across these villages on the way to Sankarakhol and Tikabali. Mula Rujangi is a little ahead of these on the same route to the right but thrown slightly back into the fields within a distance of 7 to 8 *km*. from the town. Pitabari is also located at a similar distance and in the same direction. Because of their closeness, the villages mentioned above have constant interaction with the town population and come under Verrier Elwin's class II category of tribal hamlets where village life is said to be a little individualistic because of such contact.

Villages like Sainipadar, Luhurubali and Alami cannot be approached easily since there are no proper approach roads. These are at a distance of about 9 to 10 *km* from the heart of the town. These can be approached from the opposite side to the town. One has to cross *river Pila Salunki via* a narrow bridge and wade through a few hamlets, situated by the side of the hills. Majaganda, Sarupada, Bulungi, Nuaripadar. These villages are within a distance of 10 *km* and can be approached from the college end side by a *kuchha* all-weather road running between Teraguda village and banks of *Pila Salunki.* On one's journey to these villages, one will not find roads for a good stretch of distance. One has to go by foot, mostly through fields and hills hopping over nallas and climbing on the steep gradients full of stones, big and small. Satnjargi is in the same direction within a distance of 8 *km* form the town but a different route is taken. One has to cross the river and walk through a difficult terrain for about 2 *km* before reaching the village.

A UNIT-WISE SURVEY OF THE GP

From an over-all survey of Alami GP regarding the location and character of villages, we move to a unit-survey of the separate villages.

Terguda

This village is situated on the banks of *Pila Salunki* to the right side of the main road from which it is only 1 *km* away. The approach road to the hamlet is an all-weather *kuchha* road. The village is fully electrified. But it does not have irrigation facility of any kind in spite of its proximity to the perennial water source. There are no canals, no lift irrigation points, no dug wells nor a tank. The supply of agricultural implements like pump sets and sprayers is very rare. The villagers have been provided with a sanitary well for the purpose of drinking water. The villagers have not been provided with even minimum agricultural implements such as pump sets and sprayers. However, the educational needs of the villagers are well looked after since they have easy access to the schooling facilities of all kinds available in the district headquarters. Besides, there is one adult education, centre located in the village. For a living, large number of people are engaged in making leaf-plates out of Sal leaves abundantly available in the area and some work away from the village on a daily-wage basis.

Nedipada

In Nedipada we find similar physical features, being located within 1 *km*. Distance from the main road (though official figure is 2 *km*) and in the backyard of the Government College Phulbani literally speaking. There is an all-weather *kachha* road to approach the village. The village is fully electrified, has a dug well for irrigation purpose. The children of the village are lucky to have all the schooling facilities available in the township, because of its nearness to the latter. Drinking water is available to the village from a sanitary well and a tube well provided to them.

Bandhasahi

This village comes next in terms of its physical location. It is located within a distance of 3 *km* from the town and linked to the main road by an all-weather *kachha* road. The villagers have been provided with 3 pumpsets by the Agriculture Department for the purpose of cultivation. Drinking water is available from a sanitary well and a tube well. Like the above two adjacent villages, this village too does not have a school of its own. Only one adult education centre is there for spreading literacy among the villagers. The village is not yet electrified.

Pitabari

It is located within a distance of 4 *km* from the main road with a *kuchha* all-weather link. The village boasts of a good primary school, a Mahila Samiti and, thanks to the good work of the Fisheries Department, a pisciculture tank, The villagers are engaged primarily in leaf-plate stitchling. There is provision of drinking water supplied through a sanitary well and a tube well.

Mula Rujangi

It is located within a distance of 5 *km* from the main road and 8 *km* from the middle of the town. There is an all-weather *kuchha* road to approach the village. There is neither irrigation facility nor electricity supply. Drinking water, however, has been supplied to the village through a sanitary well and a tube well. There is one pisciculture tank in the village which is in derelict condition and therefore, of no use. The village does not provide schooling facilities to its children. But there are two adult-education centres in the village. Although there is no irrigation facility, people show a great deal of interest in agriculture which is evident from large scale backyard arming — people growing vegetables, pulses, spices etc. People are engaged primarily in the household industry.

Bulungi

It is located at a distance of 7 *km* from the main road. The village does not have proper approach link though officially there is an all weather approach *kuchha* road form the main road. Except a primary school and one adult education centre and a sanitary well which is used for procuring drinking water, the village 'does not have any other facility. People are poor and primarily occupied in leaf-plate stitching. There is no supply of electricity and no irrigation facility. There are 3 pensioners under Welfare schemes living in the village.

Alami

It is the village after which the panchayat is named. Quite naturally, the village leads and is ahead of many other villages coming under Alarm G.P. It is located at a distance of 9 km from the town to which it is linked through an all-weather *kuchha* road. The village boasts of one lift irrigation point provided for the purpose of cultivation. Water from the wells and tube well is also used for irrigating small size farms. Education-wise, the village is a forward one; it has a primary school, one youth club and an adult education centre too. Suprisingly enough, the village has no supply of electricity. The chief occupations of the people are cultivation and leaf-plate making. There are a few rural artisans which is evident from the presence of a black smith's unit and a couple of carpentry units inside the village.

Nuaripadar is situated at a distance of 12 *km* from the main road. The village is linked through a fair-weather road. Like most of the villages of the G.P. this one too is deprived of basic facilities; with no irrigation facility, no schools and no supply of electricity. One comes across a pump set which is used for tapping water from the nearest source for the purpose of cultivation.

Majaganda is located at a distance of 6 *km* from the main road with an all-weather *kuchha* link from the village. People are engaged in cultivation, leaf-plate stitching, collecting forest produce etc. there is no irrigation facility, though there is occasional supply of agricultural implements such as pumpsets. The village is not provided with schooling facility; only one adult education centre is located in the village. The village is not yet electrified. One finds a number of pensioners (10 in number) in the village among the old, the disabled and the widowed who are beneficiaries under various welfare schemes.

Sarupada is located at a distance of 8 to 10 *km* from the main road with practically no road to approach the village. The chief occupation of the people is collection of forest produce apart from leaf-plate stitching. There is a carpentry unit in the village and most deprived of all villages of the GP with no facility whatsoever; not even a regular source of drinking water.

Sainipadar is located at a distance of 10 *km* from the main road with an all-weather *kuchha* link. In contrast to many villages, Sainipadar has electricity supply. Besides, it has a post office, two carpentry units, a primary school (official records have not mentioned it). The villagers have been suplied drinking water through a sanitary well. This is one of the few villages in which people take keen interest in politics.

Satanjargi is within a distance of 12 *km* from the main road. There is a fair-weather link from the main road and another fair-weather approach road from the village outwards. There are a primary school and one Mahila Samiti. Drinking water is procured from the sanitary well provided for the purpose. The main occupations of the villagers are cultivation and leaf-plate stitching. The village does not have irrigation facility nor supply of electricity.

Luhurubali which is the hot bed of local politics is located within a distance of 14 *km* from the main road and about 17 *km* from the heart of the town in the same direction as Sainipadar and Alami. The village is linked through an all-weather *kuchha* road. There are a few rural artisan families as evident from the two carpentry units and one blacksmith unit. The village is deprived of facilities of education, irrigation, supply of electricity in spite of high degree of political involvement of the villagers. There are no youth clubs, Mahila Samitis and adult education centres in the village.

A GENERAL ASSESSMENT

It is worthwhile to move from a unit-survey (of villages) to an overview of the gram panchayat infrastructure. Seen as an integrated whole, the GP presents a picture of poverty and deprivation. The population depends on the household industry and to some extent on agriculture. The income sources of people are very few, but expenditure is rising. This has pushed them into a state of indebtedness. Traditional occupations remain the mainstay of people in some parts of the GP. For instance, there are 11 carpentry units and two blacksmith units in the Panchayat area. However, there is a decline of pottery as an occupation, Bidi-making which could have been a profitable business in this Kendu growing area has virtually disappeared.

DECLINE OF AGRICULTURE

Except in one or two villages, cultivation as an occupation is treated as a liability. There are a few reasons: One, there is no irrigation facility in the entire GP in the form of irrigation projects (major or minor), no lift irrigation point except one at Alami. Two, there are constraints in the supply of the agricultural implements like power tillers, since most of the villages are without any supply of electricity. Only a few pump sets have been provided to the villagers but most of them have been discarded after being used once or twice. Villages are not competent to operate or handle these sets, either technically or knowledge wise. Three, it is difficult to market the surplus agricultural produce since there are no weekly or bi-weekly *hats* in the villages. Villagers have to travel a distance of 10 to 20 *km* by foot carrying goods to the town on the hat days, since there is no communication or transport facility. Four, surplus goods which are perishable cannot be stored since there is no cold storage facility in the GP. There are no warehouses for storing the non-perishable items. Five, there are no regular private traders to facilitate the movement of goods from the place of their origin. Six, there is no banking facility around, not a Gramya Bank, nor a cooperative bank, nor a scheduled bank. The villagers have no access to credit when they need it most.

The public distribution system is a misnomer, since one does not come across a single fair price shop in the entire GP. Animal husbandry does not figure anywhere in the occupational chart of the villagers. There is not a single diary or poultry unit in the entire GP. The GP does not have a single veterinary dispensary or a livestock centre to provide health care to the pet animals. Of course, animal health care facilities provided at the District Veterinary Hospital are available to the people from the villages which are located nearby. Pisciculture has been encouraged in a couple of villages but it has failed. The tanks are now in a moribund state. The Alami GP is industrially barren. There are no rice mills or oil mills around. There are no food processing industries which could have proved a major source of income for many villagers by processing some of their agricultural produce.

However, in at least two areas the GP is slightly better off. One, drinking water has been supplied to all villages either through sanitary wells or by sinking tube-wells. Two, the other area is education. The GP has a good literacy rate (about 53%) compared to the block and district figures. There are adult education centres in six villages to foster literacy. Besides, there are 3 Mahila Samities and two youth clubs. There are primary schools only in 5 out of 14 villages of the GP but the closeness of some villages to the town compensates for this deprivation. There are no M.E. Schools or High Schools or Ashram residential schools in the GP but the educational facilities under the block and the district administration are availed by the people. Relatively speaking, Alami, though economically one of the most backward of the GPs, is educationally not so.

IMPLEMENTATION OF THE DEVELOPMENT PROGRAMMES IN THE ALAMI GRAM PANCHAYAT

A study of the development process in the Alami GP and the extent of participation of people therein assume significance in view of the abject poverty of the villagers, absence of resources and infrastructure for industrial growth and their difficult living conditions. As we have already examined the development work undertaken by various specialised agencies in the district, it will be in the fitness of things to throw some light on the performance of these development agencies in the Phulbani Block which at present comprises 11 Gram panchayats including Alami.

THE BLOCK SCENARIO

The Phulbani Block spreads over 470 sq km with a total population of 25,516 (1981 census) out of which 13.104 are male and 12,142 are female. Originally, it was an N.E.S. block. It was a double block too, comprising both Phulbani and Khajuripada. In the year 1960, the two separate parts became two separate blocks bearing their earlier names, Phulbani Block was declared as a Tribal Development Block on 1st April 1962 and put under the Tribal Sub-Plan Area of the Integrated Tribal Development Agency. There are 213 revenue villages under the Block out of which 11 are uninhabited.

The block has a mixed population with a numerical preponderance of the Kandha tribe. Among the three segments, tribals account for 57.43%, scheduled castes for 20.44% and other castes 22.13% (1981 census). The block has a total of 5195 households living in the 202 villages. Agriculture is the chief occupation of maximum number of villagers in the Block area. The marginal farmers constitute the largest occupational category living in 3452 households

PLATE 2

MAP OF PHALBANI BLOCK

DIST - PHULBANI

SCALE = 1" 4 MILES

and the rural artisans, the smallest segment owning 64 households only. The distribution of households according to occupation is given in the following table:

Table 5.1
Occupation-wise Distribution of People in Phulbani Block

Category of Occupation	*No. of Households*	*Percentage of Households*
Small farmers	1213	23.00
Marginal Farmers	3452	66.43
Agricultural labour	246	4.73
Non-Agricultural labour	240	4.61
Rural Artisans	64	1.23
TOTAL	5195	100

As far as literacy is concerned, the block records a lower literacy percentage compared to the district. It is 26.6% in the block while the District average is 31.55%. (38.64% in the 1991cemus)

IMPLEMENTATION OF DEVELOPMENT PROGRAMMES IN THE BLOCK

The Phulbani Block, which is a Tribal Development Block witnessed considerable development drive in the 1980s in terms of infrastructure development, income and employment generation, rural rehabilitation, poverty alleviation and drought management. The major agencies of rural and tribal development working in the area are: District Rural Development Agency, Phulbani, and the Integrated Tribal Development Agency, Phulbani (the other ITDA working in the district is in the Baliguda block). The DRDA monitors the Integrated Rural Development Programme while the ITDA, Phulbani implements the Integrated Tribal Development Programme popularly known as ITDP.

Under the IRDP, a total of 2074 families of the Block (40%) were covered between 1980-81 and 1986-87 out of which 662 belonged to the Scheduled Caste and 1082, to the STs while only 330 families belonged to other castes. Under the ITDP, the total number of families assisted under various schemes in the Sixth Plan period was 396 out of which 41 belonged to the Scheduled Caste and 335 to the Scheduled Tribe. During the same period, the number of bonded labourers who were rehabilitated in the block was 162 out of which 107 were scheduled caste people and 37 were from the Scheduled Tribe and 18 belonged to other castes under the rural rehabilitation scheme popularly known as the ERRP. Monetary help was extended to 79 families in the Block by the SCSTDFCC Ltd. out of which 14 belonged to the SC and 65 to ST.

Efforts have been made to ensure employment to the rural folk under the National Rural Employment Programme (NREP), Between 1980-81 and 1987–88 assets were delivered in 266 cases. During the same period total number of mandays generated was 1,91,413. Under the housing programme (Indira Awas Yojana), construction of houses and school buildings was taken up in the the block through the combined assistance from RLEFG (Rural Landless Employment Generation Programme) and the NREP. Between 1985 to 1987, 56 houses were constructed and a school buildings was completed as part of the infrastructure development exercise with RLEGP assistance. In another phase. 85 house were constructed under the IAY with NREP assistance.

The Drought Prone Areas Programme and the ARWS Programme have been implemented in this water scarce block with good results. During one year 1986-87, 46 tube wells were sunk in some villagers of the GP which were without a regular source of drinking water. Moreover, the landless in the area have been provided with 33.97 acres of agricultural land and 0.27 acres of homestead lands.

Under different pension schemes implemented in the block, the old, the disabled and the widows have been looked after. In the area of health, the Block has not lagged behind. Under the special nutrition programme, 2100 school children have been fed through 65 primary schools free of cost. Food stuffs have been supplied to 5000 pre-school children as well as pregnant and nursing mothers through various centres under the Integrated Child Development Scheme.

THE GRAM PANCHAYAT SCENARIO

As we have mentioned before, the GP under study was created towards the end of 1991 until which it was part of the Tudipaju GP coming under the same Block—Phulbani. The villages which form part of the new GP do not form a cluster as they are scattered all over the place. Some of them are close to the Block and the District headquarters and others are at a distance, isolated and distance, isolated and de-linked from the mainland.

We have a sample of 130 families which have been assisted under various development programmes. The sample is representative as it covers 21.52% of the total number spanning all the villages of Alami GP. The number of respondents chosen from each village is approximately in the same proportion to its total population. Among the beneficiary families, there is a high percentage of tribals (69.23%) while the Scheduled Caste families constitute a relatively small percentage (25.38%). Others constitute 5.38%. The male beneficiaries outnumber the females, the former being 86.92% of the population and the latter, 13.07%. A large majority of beneficiaries covering 66.15% of the population have small families with maximum of 5 members. About 53% of them are educated at least up to the elementary level while about 47% are illiterates.

PLATE 3

MAP OF ALAMI GRAM PANCHAYAT

PHULBANI BLOCK

KHANDA MAL SUB DIVISION

DIST : PULBANI

SCALE 1 " = 1 MILE

PHULBANI N.A.C.

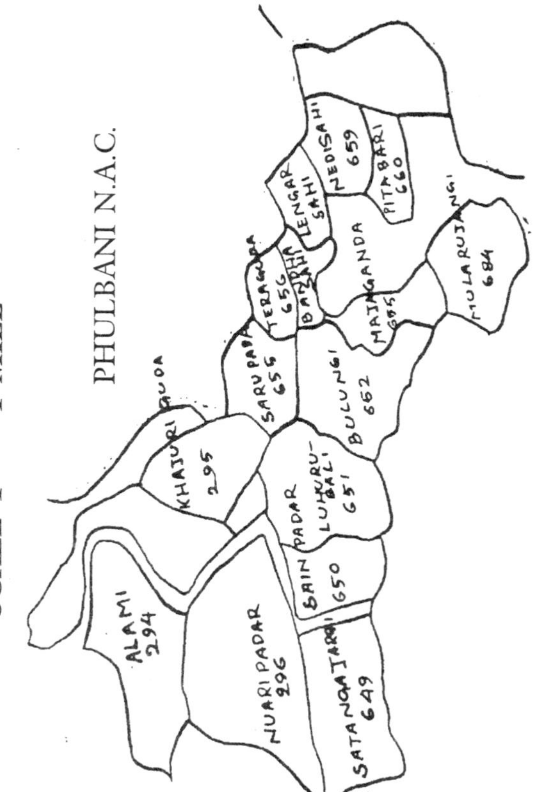

A comparative assessment reveals that the GP has received maximum development assistance under the IRDP Schemes. 55.38% of the beneficiaries have been assisted under this programme while 12.3% have been covered under the ITDP and 12.3% under the Employment and Rehabilitation of the Rural Poor popularly known as ERRP. The rest 20% have been assisted through the cooperative society and other sources combinedly. The overall picture of development in the 1980s in Alami G.P speaks of a 53.3% coverage under the three major development programmes IRDP, ITDP and ERRP. Out of the 604 families in the GP, 322 have received some benefit or the other. Out of those assisted, 183 families were covered under the IRDP while ITDP covered 50 families and ERRP covered the rest 89. The total number of scheduled caste families assisted under the three programmes was 110 while the total number of scheduled tribe families assisted was 191. Beneficiaries belonging to the other castes numbered 11 only.

Under the ERRP, 55 households have been rehabilitated in the Sixth Plan period alone. Out of those rehabilitated, 17 belong to the SC, 32 to the ST and 6 to the OC. Under another scheme of the same programme, housing sites have been provided to 60 SC families, 79 ST families and 36 other families. Ceiling surplus land has been distributed among 163 families in the GP of which 65 belong to the SC and 98 belong to the ST. There are three cases of rehabilitation of the bonded labour; one, in Teraguda village and two, in Luhurubali.

VILLAGE LIFE: ECONOMIC ORGANISATION

Tribal life is characterised by its community ethos, well-defined needs and low aspiration level. Within the means at their disposal, they lead a full life, as far as possible. They are spend-thrift. Having little concern and planning for the future, they do not feel the need either to earn more or to save.

Village is their universe. They take maximum interest in the village affairs. Material calculations of loss and profit play a small part in interpersonal relations. Soul is better and bigger than either body or mind.

The present study of Alami GP offers an interesting picture as regards the patterns of livelihood in the tribal villages. They are mostly engaged in the household industry, the most important being leaf-plate making. Women make good use of time they spend in-doors. They not only make leaf-plates (*Khali, Chowkuni* etc.) but also try to supplement family income by frying *Chuda* and *Mudhi* which they sell in various localities of the town, including the market, and in nearby weekly *hats*.

Agriculture, of course, remains one of the more stable sources of income for a good number of families. Since the crops are seasonal, farmers divert themselves to part-time work on daily wage basis. Some take to vegetable vending, if they happen to grow them in their kitchen gardens. Growing *haldi* (tamarind) in the backyard is a very common practice here.

In the relatively isolated villages situated amidst forests and hilltops, people collect firewood from forest which they sell in the town later. Those in the government jobs who are traditionally potters, weavers, blacksmiths, carpenters etc. use their leisure (vacations and off time) not only to earn a few bucks more but also to keep their traditional craft alive. There are some odd jobs like stone crushing, metal welding etc. which are quite popular among the poorer sections. Some rear goats, pigs and poultry for a living. Those living amidst forests collect the forest produce to earn their livelihood, Kendu-bush cutting, *Mahula* flower collection are also prevalent in these villages. Herding of cows and goats is also treated as a source of income by a few. In short, the tribals meet their basic needs mainly from nature. Quite appropriately, they are "simple children of nature" as some one has put it.

OCCUPATIONAL STRUCTURE

Generally, people are engaged in the following occupations; (1) agriculture (2) government services (3) daily wage labour (4) petty business and (5) household industry. Since we have come across cases where people tend to shift themselves from one occupation to the other or take up some wage work in addition to the existing one, some mixed occupational categories have come to stay. These include (i) service holders doing business (ii) cultivators doing part-time daily wage work (iii) those in business doing part-time daily-wage work. These categories have acquired a routine character, thus affecting the existing occupational patterns in the village.

Occupational categories are not merely economic/income categories; they are strong social categories also, as they give us a general idea regarding a family's economic status and life style. However in this study, we focus on occupational categories primarily as economic categories, specifically from the rural development standpoint since our objective is to discuss the development process.

The questions which need to be answered first are (1) What do we mean by development ? (2) Who is a beneficiary of development ? Development implies a few things such as: (i) alleviation of poverty (ii) creation of an infrastructure for industrial growth (iii) growth in the occupational front (iv) generation of income and employment. The prime objective of all developmental initiatives is to raise an individual's living standard or in economic parlance, to assist an individuals to cross the poverty line. In short, development aims at the economic well-being of the maximum number. A beneficiaries is one who is entitled to assistance from the government under various schemes launched through development agencies to raise the per capita family income and consequently, family's living standard. Whether somebody should be treated as a beneficiaries or not for a particular development scheme depends on a fixed criterion. The criterion of land holdings' as suggested by the National Commission on Agriculture[1] has been adopted to identity the beneficiaries.

In the commission's view, the composite projects or the agencies are to cover both small and marginal farmers having landholdings below 5 acres as well as agricultural labourers. It has defined these three categories as follows:

(*i*) **Small Farmers:** Cultivators with land holding below 5 acres. In case of Class I irrigated lands as defined under land ceiling legislation, the ceiling would be 2.5 acres.

(*ii*) **Marginal Farmers:** Cultivators having landholding up to 2.5 acres. In case of Class I irrigated land as defined under the land ceiling legislation of the state, the ceiling would be 1.25 acres.

(*iii*) **Agricultural Labourers:** Cultivators without landholding but having a homestead and deriving more than 50% of their income from agricultural wages. The above categories should include persons who are necessarily cultivators. There are 3 other categories namely (iv) rural artisans (v) non-agricultural labour and (vi) the landless in the rural development agenda of the Government.

The family/household has been taken as the unit white identifying the beneficiary and the said family unit is taken as comprising those normally living in the same household. The farmers who are eligible to be identified as beneficiaries according to the prescribed landholdings may have a good income from a source outside cultivation. Ideally, families with substantial income from off farm source should not be considered for any programme of the agencies.

The distribution of beneficiaries in the various occupation categories sampled for Alami GP is shown in the following table:

Table 5.2
Occupation-wise Distribution of the Beneficiaries in the Alami G.P.

Category	*Number*	*Percentage*
Small Farmer	21	16.1%
Marginal Farmer	58	44.6%
Rural Artisans	3	2.3%
Agricultural Labour	4	3.07%
Non-Agricultural Labour	28	21.5%
Landless	16	12.3%
Total	130	100%

From the comparison above, it may be observed (i) that the people of Alami GP are poorer in comparison to that of the other GPs of the block (ii) that importance of agriculture is declining as an occupation as suggested by the presence of a large segment of non-agricultural labourers (22%) (iii) that there is growing land alienation in the GP area as indicated by the presence of a fairly good number of landless people (12.3%).

EXTENT OF POVERTY IN THE G.P. AND THE IMPACT OF DEVELOPMENT PROCESS

It is revealed from the per capita family income survey that 87.7% of the beneficiaries are below the poverty line; their annual income from all sources remaining below Rs. 11,000. Even among this vast army of the poor, we have classified some as poor (having an annual income in the range of Rs. 3000 to Rs. 7000) and others as poorest of the poor (having an annual income below Rs. 3000).

Table 5.3
Extent of Poverty

Sl. No.	*Category*	*Income range (Rs. per annum)*	*% of Respondents*
1.	Above poverty line	11,000/- and above	12.3
2.	Poor	7000/- to 11,000/-	26.92
3.	Very poor	3000/- to 7000/-	46.16
4.	Poorest of the poor	3000/- and less	14.6
	Total		99.98

Officially, all the beneficiaries must have the below poverty line status to be eligible for assistance. In our study, 12.3% of the respondents with a reasonable annual income are shown to be above the poverty line from which it may be inferred that these beneficiaries have been able to raise their per capita family income after being assisted. Going by the response of the beneficiaries as to whether development has contributed to any rise in their living standard, 69.23% of the respondents have replied in the affirmative (See Table 6). In the first case, we have estimated the total annual income of the beneficiaries and classified them into four categories in terras of four income grades and arrived at the conclusion that development has successfully alleviated poverty in case of 12.3% of the respondents. In the second instance, we have assessed the impact in terms of a general response as given below:

Table 5.4
Rise in Living Standard

Response Category	*Respondents (%)*
Affirmative	69.24
Negative	20.76
Can't say	10
Total	100

CONSUMPTION PATTERN

The expenditure pattern suggest a certain extravagance and lack of planning on the part of villagers. Those spending up to Rs. 10,000 per annum constitute 52.3% and those spending up to Rs. 20,000 per annum constitute 44.6% and those whose expenditure exceeds RS. 20,000 are about 3.07%. The community character of people in respect of consumption pattern is not adversely affected as a result of capitalist mode of development. The expenditure incurred by the respondents on festivals and socialising testifies to the community character of the people.

Table 5.5
Community Expenditure

Expenditure (Rs. 500 per annum)	*Respondents (%)*
Festivals	80%
Socialising	83.84%

FOOD EXPENDITURE

As far as consumption of food is concerned, beneficiaries can spend maximum of Rs. 15,000 per annum. 24% of the respondents among beneficiaries spend up to Rs. 5,000 on food annually. More than 50% of the beneficiaries spend up to 10,000 per annum on this head. For some of them (20%) spend up to Rs. 15,000 per annum. Only in the case of a small minority (3.84%), such expenditure exceeds Rs. 15,000 per annum. In contrast more than 50% of the non-beneficiaries spend within Rs. 5,000 per annum. A little less than 50% of the respondents spend with in Rs. 10,000 annually on food. There are none in the two upper categories whose annual expenditure on food exceeds Rs. 10,000 and Rs. 15,000 respectively (See Table 5.6).

Table 5.6
Comparison Between Deneficiaries and Non-beneficiaries with Regard to Food Expenditure

Food expenditure per annum in Rs.	*Beneficiaries (%)*	*Non-beneficiaries (%)*
Above 15,000/-	3.84	Nil
Less than 15,000/-	20.00	Nil
Less than 10,000/-	52.30	48.14
Less than 5,000/-	23.84	51.85
Total	99.98	99.99

About 55% of the villagers are habitual takers of drink spending a minimum of Rs. 200 and maximum of Rs. 1,000 per annum while the rest abstain. This habit of the majority, though deleterious, fortifies the argument regarding their community spirit.

The villagers have very little mobility which is testified by their small expenditure towards transport. 51.53% of the respondents do not spend a pie towards transport. Entertainment outside their village such as visiting theatre etc. does not feature high in their life. It is limited only to select section. A vast majority of them (83.84%) do not spend anything in this regard. Expenditure on medicine is restricted to a maximum of Rs. 500 per annum for 80% of the respondents. This suggests two things: (i) they do not have free medical aid facility around and (ii) more and more people have become health conscious over the years so far as taking medicine is concerned. It may be stated that, in the past they depended on local methods of treatment for the cure of diseases.

DEVELOPMENT HAS RESULTED IN AGGRAVATING THE PROBLEM OF INDEBTEDNESS

The living standard has no doubt improved due to development, as this study reveals. But at the same time there is a steady rise in the debt-burden. Most of the development schemes have provisions for large credit with easy repayment facilities The propensity to depend as credit on the part of the beneficiaries has gone up while the ability to repay the debts has not. In recent years, the general perception of tribals on indebtedness has undergone a change. For a people who are hardly entrepreneurial and who have a long legacy of indebtedness, the development may prove ruinous in the long-run.

In order to find out the truth of the above observation, we made a factual survey of the performance of the respondents as far as repayment of loans is concerned. It was found that none of them has been able to repay the entire loan amount. There were those who have partially repaid (covering 47.70%) and others who have not repaid at all covering about the same number (46.92%). Besides, there was a small section of beneficiaries (5.38%) who did not actually avail themselves of any loan (See Table 5.7).

The reasons for default were many. 18.46% were reluctant to repay as they were expecting a loan-waiver (which the populist governments have done in the past). An equal percentage of the respondents attributed it to financial pressure, 11.53% of the beneficiaries said that they could not get loan due to some reason such as old age, sickness etc. and therefore repayment was out of question. In this particular response, we find a marked percentage rise compared to a similar response earlier. (from 5.38% to 11.53%) which may be due to the presence of some dodgers among respondents who chose to hide facts. Cases of wilful defaulting are limited to 6.92%. The predominant reason given, however, was 'meeting of immediate and outstanding consumption needs'. (44.33%) (See Table 10). The high degree of default proves our point that the development process indirectly has contributed to the rising incidence of indebtedness.

Table 5.7
Repayment Status of the Loanee

Sl. No.	*Category*	*Respondent (%)*
1.	Partially repaid	47.70
2.	Not repaid at all	46.92
3.	Not actually availed a loan	5.38
	Total	100

Table 5.8
Reasons of Non-repayment/Default

Sl. No.	*Response Category*	*Respondent (%)*
1.	Expected loan waiver	18.46
2.	Financial pressure	18.46
3.	Spent on immediate and outstanding consumption needs	44.63
4.	Wilful default	6.92
5.	Not availed due to some reason	11.53
	Total	100

Although the tribals under study are poor and thus entitled to a number of benefits under various development schemes, most of them are not aware of this owing to their low literacy level and lack of access to information. Added to these, there is the problem of immobility which cuts off the tribals from the rest of the world. Moreover, there are a host of officials to be approached, a lot of formalities to be completed and quite a few financial transactions to be made through the bank before the actual procurement of benefits. All these require a high degree of competence on the part of beneficiaries which the tribals so conspicuously lack. How then, do the benefits reach them ? Who links them to the administration ?

Since this is a key aspect in the whole exercise, it was taken up as a part of our survey. The respondents revealed that the village level workers (VLWs) are the most useful link between them and the administration in this regard. According to 68.46% of them, the VLWs are the most trusted ones and the most easily available. 17.69% have tried on their own. In a few cases (2.3%), local politicians and in a few others cases, Village Agricultural Workers (1.53) have been of some help. About one-tenth of the respondents have received help from miscellaneous sources. The following table gives the percentage distribution of various sources of help:

Table 5.9
Assistance Procurement Link

Sl. No.	*Category*	*Respondents (%)*
1.	Local Politicians	2.3
2.	Village Level Workers	68.46
3.	Village Agricultural Workers	1.53
4.	Self	17.69
5.	Miscellaneous	10.02
	Total	100

IS DEVELOPMENT A GOVERNMENT MONOPOLY?

In spite of the presence of a large number of Non-Government Organisations working in the Kandhamal District, the Government remains the development leader. The NGOs are mostly engaged in areas such as non-formal education, environmental awareness promotion, prohibition etc. But their direct contribution to the economic development is far too limited compared to the Government. The overall response to our questions on the relative usefulness of funding agencies shows that the central government remains the most valuable agency. The NGOs score badly in the popularity test. 92% of the respondents are not even aware of the Non-Governmental Organisations (NGOs). It is further revealed from the survey that the performance of the government officials at the block and district levels has been more or less satisfactory as 56.1% of the respondents speak in their favour.

WHAT SHOULD BE THE DEVELOPMENTAL PRIORITY?

In a test of developmental priority, it was observed that agriculture and allied areas scored over the other areas as 15.3% considered these to be the priority areas. Supply of electricity to all villages is treated as a pre-requisite for development by 8% of them. Housing is given priority by 6% of the respondents and health by 4%. One-tenth of the population consider public distribution system and provision of civic amenities to be the foci of development. A very large segment of the population (46%) adopted a passive attitude towards development.

CONCLUSION

The analysis of the panchayat data amply proves that the process of development has made a positive contribution to the standard of living of the tribals. It has led to an accretion of their annual income as well as enhancement in their spending capacity. The comparison between the beneficiaries and non-beneficiaries as regards their total annual income and total annual expenditure testifies to the fact.

Comparing annual per capita family income of the beneficiaries, with that of the non-beneficiaries we find that there is a greater number of beneficiaries (12.3%) above the poverty line compared to the non beneficiaries (3.7%) enjoying the similar economic status. The comparison between the two groups belonging to the other income categories shows that the percentage presence of the poor and poorest in the ranks of beneficiaries and non-beneficiaries is just about the same, while the percentage of the very poor among the latter is of a greater extent (55.55%) compared to that among the former (46.16%). Table 5.10 shows the comparative annual income profiles of the beneficiaries and non-beneficiaries.

Table 5.10
Comparative Income Profile of Beneficiaries and Non-beneficiaries

Sl. No.	*Total Annual Income (in Rupees)*	*Beneficiaries % out of 130*	*Non-beneficiaries % out of 65*
1.	Above poverty line	12.3	3.7
2.	Less than 11,000/-	26.92	25.92
3.	Less than 7,000/-	46.16	55.55
4.	Less than 3,000/-	14.6	14.81
	Total	99.98	99.98

Table 5.11
Comparative Consumption Profile of Beneficiaries and Non-beneficiaries

Sl. No.	*Total Annual Expenditure*	*Beneficiaries %*	*Non-beneficiaries %*
1.	Upper limit Rs. 10,000	52.30	88.88
2.	Upper limit Rs. 20,000	44.61	11.11
3.	Upper limit Rs. 30,000	03.07	Nil
	Total	99.98	99.99

Further, if one looks at the total annual consumption expenditure and draws a comparison, on its basis, between the beneficiaries and non-beneficiaries, it will be evident that former are economically better off than the latter (See Table 5.11). Judged form the standpoints of both income and consumption, the beneficiaries clearly enjoy a better economic status than the non-beneficiaries.

REFERENCE

1. See *Report of the National Commission on Agriculture* (New Delhi, Ministry of Agriculture: Government of India, 1976).

6
POLITICAL PARTICIPATION

WHAT IS POLITICAL PARTICIPATION?

Political participation is the heart of all democracies, although it is common to all societies; 'primitive', 'transitional' and 'modem'. It refers to the extent to which individuals are involved at various levels in the political system. It covers a whole range of political and quasi-political activities and is applicable to all types of political systems. The form and nature of participation may vary from one political system to other depending on the extent to which the individual receives political stimuli, the individual's personal and social characteristics and the political setting or environment in which the individual finds himself.[1]

NATURE OF TRIBAL PARTICIPATION: ATTITUDE AND ENVIRONMENT

Our focus in this chapter is political participation in a 'traditional primitive' society where several factors restrict and condition participation. The tribals living in this society have typical social characteristics which influence their political behaviour. Politics does not fascinate them. The messy nature of politics, the complex human equations that prevail in political bargaining and the absence of ethical considerations in political life frighten them very much. Further, they live in a society which hardly encourages political participation. It provides an integrated social and political environment in which it is extremely difficult to differentiate between political and non-political activities. In contrast, the more developed societies provide for a relatively flexible social system and a political environment which is ideal for political participation.

In spite of the several limitations—social and environmental-political participation is acknowledged by tribals as important since it is the key to their growth and self-assertion as a community and otherwise. Politics is a modern artifice and adapting to it is a great challenge for them. In the last fifty years, or so, they have had considerable political education in the form of participation in electoral process. Going by the data available, one cannot but confess that a process of gradual assimilation of tribals into the mainstream has been taking place over the years.

INDICES OF PARTICIPATION

Indices of participation and their relative importance vary from one system to the other. Voting, of course, is the most obvious index of political participation but it is hardly the most reliable. Political sociologists like Dowse and Hughes regard voting as the least active form of political participation since it requires a minimal commitment which ceases once the vote is cast. Moreover, it depends on the frequency of elections. Environmental factors also influence voting turnout. According to S. M. Lipset these are: (*i*) whether the election is taking place at a time of crisis (*ii*) the extent to which policies of the government are relevant to the individual (*iii*) the extent to which the individual has access to relevant information, among others.[2]

In this chapter, we propose to examine the extent of tribal political participation. For this purpose, we have selected besides, voting, a few important variables namely, political inclination, political awareness, political perception, political perspicacity effectiveness etc. These variables help us to understand political participation as a multidimensional process. Before we take up a discussion of the various dimensions it is worthwhile to ponder if it is relevant in the context of apparent political apathy.

ARE THE TRIBALS POLITICALLY APATHETIC?

Our survey in the Alami Gram Panchayat reveals that 71.5% of the beneficiary population are disinterested in politics. On the face of it, this indicates that majority of the tribals who are beneficiaries of various developmental programmes are politically apathetic but it confirms to our general observation of the tribal traits. Tribals apparently do not show any interest in politics. The question is whether this is by choice or because of factors beyond their control. One may legitimately argue that such disinterestedness is due to a certain dissatisfaction with the way politics is practiced. In this sense, they are rather alienated. Political participation does not necessarily presuppose acceptance of the political system and alienation may manifest through political activity as well as inactivity.

Going by the turnout during elections one may dare to refute our argument. For example, about 97% of the respondents have voted in the 1990-91 General Elections to the Parliament, the Elections to the Orissa Legislative Assembly that year, and the G.P elections (Alami G.P) around the same time. How is this possible if only 28.5% are politically interested? The right answer probably is that they have no choice but to vote. They keep voting and keep hoping. Time and again, they elect governments which fail them, belie their hopes, forget their promises which they made before elections. Accumulated dissatisfaction has turned their faith (in the system, in the elected political leaders) into distrust and aversion. In a true sense, therefore, they are alienated and not apathetic as many including tribals themselves would make us believe. The large negative response with regard to interest in politics was partly due to the fact that the question put to them was rather direct and blunt.

TRENDS IN TRIBAL POLITICAL PARTICIPATION

In our study, tribal political participation is viewed as a comprehensive process encompassing the political activities not only of the tribals but also those belonging to the scheduled caste or other castes living in the tribal area, because one does not find a significant deviation from the majority norm. However, at times, there have been departures from the majority norm, which we have taken note of in order to highlight the newly emerging trends in the tribal political participation and their implications for social change.

One can discern a few clear trends in the tribal political participation from a study of the results of the 1995 Assembly elections. In the three Assembly constituencies of the district—Baliguda, Udayagiri, Phulbani, there was a large number of independent candidates contesting the elections. In Baliguda, four out of nine candidates, in Udayagiri, three out of six candidates and in Phulbani, four out of eight candidates were independent candidates. Secondly, the percentage of polling in all the three Assembly constituencies was very high (more than 77%) in Baliguda it was 77.30%, in Udayagiri, 79.07% and in Phulbani. 77.49%. It may be mentioned here that assembly constituencies of Baliguda and Udayagiri are reserved for the tribals while Phulbani. for the scheduled caste. In spite of this, the percentage of turnout in all the three was just about the same. Thirdly, if we go by the voting percentage genderwise, we notice a striking similarity in all the three constituencies. The participation rate of the male voters was about 40% (40.79 in Baliguda, 40.07 in Udayagiri. 40.88 in Phulbani) while that of the female voters was a little less. The turnout of female voters was slightly higher in Udayagiri

(39%) compared to other two assembly constituencies where it was about 36% (36.51 in Baliguda and 36.61 in Phulbani). Fourthly, in Baliguda and Phulbani constituencies the winning candidates got about 37% of the popular vote (37.40% and 36.59% respectively) while in Udayagiri the winner got 49.73% showing a higher degree of participation in the latter.

The only departure from the major trends in participation was found in the Phulbani assembly constituency in the aftermath of 1994 communal conflict between the tribals and scheduled caste people[3]. Here no national parties contesting the elections could win. One independent candidate representing the new tribal formation KVP *(Kandhamala Vikash Parishad)* came out successful, though with a small margin. This was an exception rather than the rule.

ELECTORAL PARTICIPATION

Voting as Participation

We first take up political participation in terms of voting keeping in mind that it is not always an act of choice, hardly so in case of tribals. The right to vote is undoubtedly the most important political right which a democratic citizen is bestowed on since the making/unmaking of a government is directly linked to the way it is exercised. Indirectly, it affects the society as well. As we are all aware, our rigid hierarchical social system has been under pressure to change towards more egalitarian goals as a consequence of mass participation.

Contesting Elections is another form of electoral participation and is considered more important than other kinds of participation since those contesting elections are concerned with the exercise of formal political power. From the point of view of the candidates and from the point of view of group or section he comes from, the right to contest election assumes particular significance since it confers on him and the group the access to power.

Besides there are other forms of political participation linked to elections: Canvassing or campaigning for particular leaders or parties and attending meetings of various political parties. All these four forms of participation are specially relevant during elections and can rightly be called electoral participation.

WHAT IS THEN, THE NATURE AND EXTENT OF POLITICAL PARTICIPATION AMONG TRIBALS?

In order to examine the nature and extent of electoral participation, we have confined ourselves to the 1990-91 General Elections to the Parliament, the Assembly Polls and the GP Elections held in the same year and tested the participation rate at the national, state and local level with the help of four variables mentioned above.

Table 6.1
Rate of Electoral Participation (Except Voting)

	Category of activity	*Respondents(%)*
1.	Contested	26.93
2.	Canvassed	34.61
3.	Attended Political Meetings	38.46
	Total	100

With regard to voting, 97% of the respondents said that they have voted in all the three Elections. But, it will be naive to conclude that participation rate is nearly one hundred percent. This is not so anywhere in the world, not even in the most mature democracies. We get a more realistic picture about the extent of political participation using the other three variables. 26.92% of the respondents have contested in one of the three elections mentioned above. 34.61% have canvassed during elections on behalf of political parties while

38.46% attended political meetings during the election year. The above table gives the rate of political participation in the electoral activities linked to voting.

Tribals as Induced Voters

Are the tribals making good use of their right to franchise? The preceding discussion reveals that it is actually not so. The reason is: Tribal voters are generally poor, illiterate, uninformed and without a system of communication. There are several factors which motivate them to set up a march to the poling booth and cast their vote. We have listed a few factors of motivation and solicited their response as to who has motivated them to vote.

It is found that strong kinship bond is a powerful factor guiding them to vote which is a case with 28.46% of the respondents. Village elders influence 10.76% of them to vote one way or the other. Leaders of various political parties influence 15.38% of the respondents. Money does not play as a significant role as it does elsewhere. 6.15% of the population are guided by the lure of money. Youth clubs are yet to acquire a political role in this regard. A sizeable number come in the category of self-conscious voters constituting 28.46% of the respondents. In some cases (10.76%) a combination of two or three factors influence voting (see Table 6.2 below):

Table 6.2
Motivation Level

Motivator	*Motivated(%)*
Kinsmen	28.46
Village elders	10.76
Political Leaders	15.38
Money	6.15
Self	28.46
A combination of factors	10.76
Total	99.97

HOW MUCH POLITICALLY INCLINED ARE THEY?

It is very much established that voting is a less reliable form of political participation than other political activities i.e., political inclination, for instance, is one. Moreover, political sociologists have shown that there is a considerable gap between voter turnout and the level of interest shown by the people in different contexts. Political inclination, one may presume, is an ideal precondition to active participation. Relying on this presumption we have made an attempt to measure it in the case of tribals of an Orissan district by asking two questions:

1. Whether they are interested in village affairs?
2. Whether they are affiliated to any specific political party?

The objective is to find out different types of political participation on the basis of their political inclination.

(*i*) Whether it is 'diffuse' sort of participation.

(*ii*) Whether it is 'specific' political participation suggesting specific political involvement.

A positive response to the first question implies that they have a general interest in community affairs in which case political participation is diffuse. In other words, they are participating, though in a quasi-political way. In our survey of the Alami Gram Panchayat we find that 90% of the respondents take positive interest in village affairs. A positive response to the second question regarding their party affiliation means that the nature of participation is specific rather than diffuse. Our survey reveals that 23% of the respondents are members of one political party or the other (See Table below). Thus the rate of political participation as indicated by political inclination extends to 90% in the diffuse type and to 23% in the 'specific' type.

Table 6.3
Level of Political Inclination

Type of Inclination	*Respondents (%)*
Diffuse	90
Specific	23

DO THEY HAVE A POLITICAL PREFERENCE?

The third variable, in our variables series is political preference to assess the extent of political participation. Our question in this regard was; which type (Congres-led or Janta-led) of government do they prefer, one, at the centre, two, in the state. Indirectly, this is intended to know if they are ideologically oriented. In a relative sense, the Congress party believes in a authoritarian style of functioning while Janata Dal stands for democratic decentralisation. We have deliberately discounted the fact that some respondents may not be quite conscious of the underlying import of the question, while responding, except in a vague way.

The nature of participation assessed on the basis of political preference is critical and therefore we may call it critical participation. In the first case, that is, at the centre, 28.46% of the respondents prefer a Congres-led government, while 6.15% want a Janata-led government. Some are critical of both (11.53%). A majority (53.86%) failed to respond. However, the general response in the second case regarding their political preference in the state is more positive and a little more crystallised but along the same lines. 37.69% of the respondents prefer a Congress-led government while 16.92% want a Janata Dal-led government. The number of disillusioned respondents not happy with either Congress Party or Janta Dal extend, to 8.46% while those who expressed their inability to respond are 36.92%. The comparative preference can be seen from the table 6.4.

Table 6.4
Extent of Political Participation on the Basis of Political Preference

Sl. No.	*Category of Preference*	*Respondents(%)*	
		At the centre	*In the state*
i.	Want a Congress government	28.46	36.69
ii.	Want a Janata Dal-led government	6.15	16.92
iii.	Want neither Congress nor Janata	11.53	8.46
iv.	Can't Say	53.86	36.92
	Total	100	100

The above discussion highlights the following facts:

(*i*) Diffuse participation extends to 90%

(*ii*) Specific participation covers only 23%

(*iii*) Critical participation extends to 15.37% and 21.02% at the national and state level respectively.

What is the Extent of Political Awareness of the Tribals?

Political awvareness is the fourth variable of political participation in our scheme. This is also an ideal prerequisite for participation. Questions on political awareness are intended to test the respondents' awareness of politics at three levels; national, state and local level. They pertain to information/knowledge regarding the constitution of India, the President of India, concerned Member of the Parliament, concerned member of the Legislative assembly and his contributions, village Sarpanch, the Gram Panchayat, the Election Commission of India and the photo-identity card introduced by the Former Election Commissioner, Mr. T.N. Seshan.

It is observed that except in one specific case, the awareness of tribals about the national level politics is rather dismal. Only 2.3% of the respondents know that we have a constitution and 3.07% of them are aware of the President of India. 20.76% are familiar with their M.P. and have information about his visits to the village. In our survey, Seshan, the Ex-Election Commissioner of India emerges a national hero because of his charismatic qualities drawing a positive response from 80%. Regarding his contribution i.e. introduction of the Photo-Identity Card for the voter, 46.69% of the respondents feel that it is a positive step while 43.84% have no idea of what it is.

The level of political awareness of respondents with regard to state politics is better compared to national level politics. Political leaders (state-level), such as the local MLA, are known throughout the villages. 95% of the respondents are familiar with their MLA. However, regarding MLA's specific contribution, only 65.38% offer a positive response.

The level of awareness about local politics, is fairly good. 80% of the respondents are familial with the local political leaders like the Sarpanch. However, direct involvement with the activities of the Gram Panchayat is limited to 25.38% of the respondents. Only a miniscule minority (1.53%) have an intimate knowledge of the GP i.e. its sources of funding etc. The following table gives a picture of comparative awareness level:

Table 6.5
Level of Political Awareness

Sl. No.	*Category of Awareness*	*Respondents(%)*		
		National level	*State level*	*Local level*
1.	Personalities			
	(a) Representative Political leaders.	20.76	95	80
	(b) Charismatic National leaders	80	-	-
2.	Political Affairs	2.3 to 3	65.38	25.38

At the end of the awareness survey, we find that the extent of participation in the form of political awareness is greater at the state level compared to the other two levels. The level of awareness about political personalities is higher than the same with regard to political affairs at all the three levels.

DO THEY HAVE A VIEW OF POLITICS?

We now turn to another determinant of political participation, namely, political perception; how do tribals perceive politics. It is their perception of people and events which determine their response to the stimuli they receive. As Milbrath points out, one of the major factors of political participation is the extent to which the individual receives political stimuli or the extent to which he engages in political activity. Political perception conditions his response to politics in general and political participation in particular.

Table 6.6
Extent of Participation on the Basis of Political Perception

Sl. No.	*Category*	*Type*	*Respondent %*
1.	Doing politics as a profession	Professional	4.6
2.	Promoting self-interests	Machiavellian	NIL
3.	Following the village bosses	'Ram' Type	23.07
4.	Politics is a game of the crooks	Cynical	5.38
5.	Promoting common interest through politics	Ideal	0.76
6.	Politics is an expression of general/community will	Communitarian	19.23
7.	Meeting basic needs through politics	Minimal	10
8.	We have no idea about/ no interest in politics	Non-Political	36.92

But do the tribals have definite perception of politics. The answer can be YES; and it can be NO too. In a "traditional primitive" society[4] where political activity is closely integrated with general social activity, it is difficult to say that the individual has a clear political perception. It is possible to argue they have 'group' minds. We have not however, ruled out the idea that tribals do have a political perception, though in a cruder form. We have placed before the respondents eight different statements representing the ways in which politics can possibly be viewed and corresponding to each one of them, we have a type of political man.

In the above table, we have tried to evolve a typology based on eight categories of political perception and recorded the respondents' views against each. Those who regard politics as their full-time occupation are professionals constituting 4.61% of the respondents. There was no representative for the Machiavellian type for whom politics is a means of self-promotion, 23.07% of the respondents believe that they have to obey what the elderly bosses in the village command and quite befittingly, they are the 'Ram' type. In contrast to this, there is the cynical type which views politics as a game of the crooks and scoundrels with a share of 5.38%. It is rare to find the ideal type which subscribes to the view that politics is intended to promote common welfare as this type is represented by 0.76% of the respondents. According to the communitarian type, politics is the expression of general will and the respondents subscribing to this view constitute 19.23% of the total population studied. Those who perceive politics as a means to meet the basic needs of life are about one-tenth of the population. A significant percentage of the population (37%) belong to the non-political type showing no interest in politics whatsoever. The 3D pie-diagram below brings out the percentage share of each of the 8 types.

Beneficiary Typology Based On Political Perception

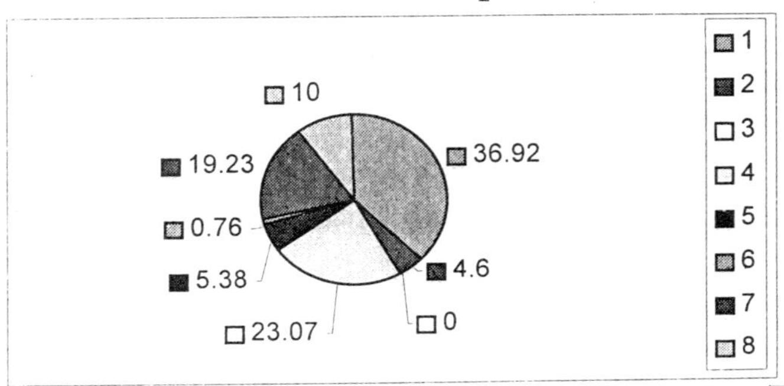

1. Non-Political 2. Professional 3. Machlavellan 4. Ram Type 5. Cynical 6. Ideal 7. Communitarian 8. Minimal

DO THEY HAVE THE CRITICAL ABILITY TO ASSESS POLITICAL EVENTS AROUND THEM?

Conscious participation necessarily involves some ability on the part of individuals to understand and critically assess the political developments around them. This is referred to as political perspicacity in the present study. It may be defined as one's ability to observe, understand and critically assess the political happenings around him. In short, it is the power of probity. We have measured the extent of participation using the respondents' probity power by asking them questions on an important political development in the Kandhamal district and its impact on the electoral process.

The questions were:

(*i*) Did the communal tension (the prolonged tribe-caste conflicts of 1994) affect the results of the 1995 Assembly polls which took place in the midst of it?

(*ii*) Were the polls qualitatively any different from the previous polls?

The response, surprisingly enough, was very encouraging. A good number of the respondents (47.69%) held that the communal tension affected the poll results. A greater number

(67.69%) was of the view that it was significantly different from the rest of the polls that had taken place earlier.

Table 6.7
Level of Probity

Sl. No.	*Level of Probity*	*Respondents(%)*
1.	1994 Communal conflict affected result of the Assembly Polls of 1995.	47.69
2.	1995 Assembly Polls were qualitatively different from previous polls.	67.69

It is evident that the people of the GP in general possess significant amount of political perspicacity which might have positive impact on their political participation.

WHAT IS THE NATURE AND EXTENT OF POLITICAL PARTICIPATION AT THE GRASS-ROOT LEVEL? : THE TRENDS

Our survey has already revealed that tribal awareness and general involvement with regard to state politics is greater than is the case with regard to politics either at the national or local level. Voting turnout remaining just about constant at all the three levels, the allied electroral activities constitute the areas where the relative intensity of participation can be measured. We have chosen one, out of three allied electoral activities: attendance in political meetings and tried to ascertain the rate of frequency in such attendance, at the grass-root level. We have recorded earlier that the general attendance in political meetings during election time is 38.46%.

It is important to find out the frequency of participation in such meeting at the grass-root level in order to as certain the participation of respondents. It is at this level that crucial decisions are taken in the two local bodies: Gram Sabha and Gram Panchayat, which affects the villagers directly. The frequency of respondents' attendance in the meetings of these two bodies has been recorded. Those who always attend the Gram Sabha meetings constitute 35.38% of the population. Those attending such meetings selectively are 41.53% while those who attend rarely are 6.15%. About 17% of the respondents abstain from such meetings.

In case of the Gram Panchayat, the local elective body, those who always attend its meetings are a meagre 3.07%. Those who attend some times constitute only 4.62%. An equally small segment of the population (4.62%) rarely attend such meetings while a vast majority (87.69%) abstain.

The comparative frequency of political participation in respect of attending local meetings can be seen from the table below:

Table 6.8
The Attendance Frequency at the Grass-root Level

Sl. No.	*Frequency of attendance in political meetings*	*Participants (%)*		*Total*
		Gram Sabha	*Gram Panchayat*	
1.	Attend always	35.38	3.07	38.45
2.	Attend sometimes	41.53	4.62	46.15
3.	Attend rarely	6.15	4.62	10.77
4.	Don't attend at all	16.94	87.69	104.63
	Total	100.00	100.00	200.00

From the above comparison, one will notice a sharp contrast in people's attitude towards the two local bodies. The total attendance in the meetings of the Gram Sabha, which is the General body of the village, is 83.08% suggesting a mass orientation in the first case. The total participation in the G.P. meetings is restricted to 12.29% of the population which is much lower than the general rate of participation. The state level and national political meetings attract a much larger segment than those at the local level in electoral terms.

In other words, political participation at the higher level of politics is greater than the political participation at the grass-roots level in terms of attendance frequency.

IS THERE A SPECIFIC MOTIVE BEHIND POLITICAL PARTICIPATION?

From the preceding discussion, it is revealed that tribals engage themselves in political activities where they regard these as useful. The extent of political participation is determined by their personal and social characteristics as well as the political and social environment. Party politics is not encouraged by the tribals in their immediate surroundings in their locality or village and their involvement in it is restricted to the elections. This reflects not only their social characteristics but also their priorities with regard to political involvement. With regard to social characteristics as a factor of political participation, 62% of the respondents held that party politics in the village does not affect them at all; further, community involvement is preferred to political involvement in the locality and in the village. As shown earlier, 90% of the respondents take positive interest in village affairs. Politics is not encouraged even in the local elective bodies. Abstention of 87.69% of the respondents from Gram Panchayat meetings corroborates this fact. Moreover, the overall picture of political participation also shows that the respondents attach less importance to grass-root politics in comparison to state level and national level politics.

Political participation has certain specific functions, firstly, as a means of pursuing economic needs; secondly, as a means of satisfying a need for social adjustment; thirdly, as a means of pursuing particular values, and fourthly, as a means of meeting subconscious and psychological needs[5]. In our study, political participation has the second and third functions. This is evident from the responses of the respondents as detailed below Almost all vote but not for the same reason.

(*a*) There are those who consider voting their right (14.6%).

(*b*) There are others who are guided (17.6%).

(*c*) Some go by a standard pattern while voting (20.6%).

(*d*) A section considers voting as an act of civic consciousness and a duty (15.2%).

(*e*) Another section sees the act as a means to good government and better life (8.4%).

(*f*) Some vote as if it is a ritual to be performed (16.7%).

(*g*) 7.7% of the respondents vote for a combination of several considerations.

Some sections are quite conscious of the motives of their participation [categories (a), (d) & (e)] and qualify to be called conscious participants in politics. There are those who participate in a mechanical way (category-f) and the rest [categories (b), (c) & (g)] are just guided. Accordingly, there are three kinds of political participation based on motives (See Table 6.9).

Table 6.9
Rate of Participation Based on Motives

Type of Participation	*Categories of Respondents (%)*	*Total (%)*
Mechanical	16.7 (f)	16.7
Conscious	14.6(a) +15.2(d) +18.4(e)	38.2
Guided	17.6(b) +20.6(c) +7.7(g)	45.1
Total	100	100

The motives of action in a traditional society are influenced by the behavioural norms of a social group to which the individual belongs. The type of political participation which results from this pattern of behaviour is mechanical political participation. But this is not borne out by the present study. The tribals take port in politics not only in mechanical manner, but also consciously. Some of them are also encouraged to do so by the village leaders/elders.

IS THEIR POLITICAL PARTICIPATION EFFECTIVE?

Effectiveness[6] in the modern world means primarily economic development. But political participation should not only be a means of pursuing economic needs, it should also ensure to the people a few other things in order to be effective. These are (*i*) equitable access to health and other aspects of physical well-being (*ii*) equitable access to knowledge, skills, technology and information (*iii*) equal access to human rights.[7] The other aspect of effective participation is that there should not be obstacles to people's access to these things. The obstacles[8] may lie either in the legal system or in the administrative rules and procedures. They may arise out of uneven distribution of income and assets. Furthermore, rigid social norms and values may also come in the way as stumbling blocks.

The point then is: do the people have the scope to redress their grievances whenever and wherever they are deprived of their rightful claims. Questions were asked to the villagers regarding the use of options available to them in this regard in order to assess the extent of effective political participation. 28.4% of the respondents trust that their village elders, if approached, will help solve their problems. A greater percentage (34.6%) prefer to approach their respective ward members or Sarpanch. Surprisingly, the concerned MLA is rarely approached while the concerned MP enjoys the confidence of 5.38% of the respondents. However, respondents ruled out the idea of making an approach to the police or going to the court. A reasonable number of people (15.38%)

approach the officials at the block level, while 15.52% of them are resigned to their fate. The following table speaks of the rate of effective political participation[9] in terms of grievance redressal:

Table 6.10
Rate of Effective Political Participation on the Basis of Grievance Redressal

Sl. No.	*Level of Grievance Redressal*	*Respondents (%)*
1.	Village Elders	28.40
2.	Local Political	34.60
3.	M.L.A.	0.72
4.	M.P.	5.38
5.	Police	Nil
6.	Courts	Nil
7.	Officials	15.38
8.	None	15.52
	Total	100.00

It appears from the above table that village-level (1&2) redressal is most widely preferred followed by official level redressal. This indicates that they generally look for a proximate redressal centre. The low rate of redressal at the level of elected leaders like MLA and the MP is due to the fact they are not available most of the time. The total absence of redressal at the levels of police and the courts may be due to the fear of the police and the complex legal procedures respectively. It may also be because the respondents are averse to the colonial style of governance. To put it more succinctly, the rate of redressal at the village level is 63% under category 1&2, while this is restricted to 6.1% at the political level under category 3 & 4 and to 15.38% at the official level under category 7 respectively. Redressal is altogether extinct at the levels of police and the courts while it is absent in the case of 15.52%

of the respondents. Going by Lipset's definition, effective political participation means how many respondents feel satisfied with the system as represented by the officials, the police and the courts as far as grievance redressal goes. In this study, the total extent of effective political participation is 15.38%.

IS DEVELOPMENT A FACTOR OF ACCELERATING THE RATE OF POLITICAL PARTICIPATION?

This is a difficult question to answer because of two reasons; Firstly, the rate of change in political participation is not noticeable in the voting turnout which remains constant in spite of the changes that take place and in this sense, it can hardly be treated as a reliable indicator of political participation. Secondly, in different contexts, which we have examined already, gain in economic terms is not a great factor of inducement for the voter nor does it constitute a motive for political participation.

One may only conjecture that a rise in the living standard of the people as a consequence of economic development attracts more people ro participate in political activities; that political participation is conditioned by economic development, at least to some extent. As we have examined earlier, development implies a marked improvement in the living standard. Hence there may be no harm in using the two terms 'development' and 'Better Living standard' interachangeably, for the sake of our analysis.

The study shows that developmental assistance produces positive impact on the political participation of the beneficiaries. Those who are more active in the post-assistance phase constitute 19.23% of the respondents. The percentage share of the politically active population was 16.15% in the pre-assistance phase. The study was diachronic; done in two phases to bring out the difference in the rates of political participation.

Table 6.11
Rate of Change in Political Participation As a Consequence of Development

Political participation in the pre-assistance	*Political participation in the post-assistance*	*Rate of change in political participation*
Phase (1)	Phase (2)	(3) 2 – 1
16.15%	19.23%	3.08% (+)

The change in the rate of political participation is difference between the rate of participation the post-assistance phase (2) and that of the pre-assistance phase (1) which is to say 3=(2) – (1). The result of the analysis shows that there is a positive rise, though small in the rate of political participation as a result of economic development.

NON-BENEFICIARY TRIBAL POLITICAL PARTICIPATION IN POLITICS

Although our focus is on the study of the interface between development and political participation in the case of the beneficiary tribals, we have undertaken a parallel study of the nature of political participation in the case of those tribals who have not been sanctioned any governmental assistance for development: the non-beneficiaries. The objective is to compare and contrast the two patterns of political behaviour in the context of development using the same set of political variables. Since we have already examined the nature and extent of political participation of the beneficiaries in the preceding sections of the chapter, here we concentrate on the participation of the tribal non-beneficiaries.

As far as voting is concerned, the over all turn-out of the non-beneficiaries is as impressive as that of the beneficiaries in the elections at various levels. In the case of the former, the turn out rate in the 1995 Assembly election is 96.2% while it is 97% in case of the latter. At the grass-roots level and the national level, however, the beneficiaries have shown greater degree of involvement than the non-beneficiaries though the turn-out rate is very high in both cases. The comparison between the two cases is given in the following table:

Table 6.12
Comparison Between Rates of Voting Turn-out of the Beneficiaries and the Non-beneficiaries

Level of Voting	*Turn-out of the Beneficiaries (% out of 130)*	*Turn-out of the Non-Beneficiaries (% out of 65)*
G.P.	97	88.8
Assembly	97	96.2
Parliament	97	88.5

The participation of beneficiaries in the polls as shown in the table is uniformly high while the rate of non-beneficiaries participation at the state level is higher in comparison to their participation at the grass-roots and national levels.

Coming to the allied electoral activities such as canvassing, contesting and attending political meetings, we find that the beneficiaries participation in these activities is much higher than the participation of non-beneficiaries. Beneficiary respondents who attended political meetings constitute an impressive 38.46% as against a low rate of participation (11%) by the non-beneficiaries. In the matter of contesting elections, the beneficiaries (26.92%) have shown a great deal of interest while the non-beneficiaries' interest in such activity is zero. Again in the matter of canvassing before election the participation rate of the beneficiaries (34.61%) is way above that of the non-beneficiaries (11%). The comparison between the two cases is given in the table.

Table 6.13
Comparative Participation in the Allied Electoral Activities

Type of Participation	*Beneficiaries (% out of 130)*	*Non-beneficiaries (% out of 65)*
Canvassing	34.61	11
Contesting	26.92	Nil
Attending Political meetings	38.46	11

As far as the activities indicating political inclination are concerned, the beneficiaries have been found to be far more politically inclined than the non-beneficiaries. The interest of non-beneficiaries in village affairs is restricted to only 51.8% of the respondents and their affiliation to political parties is restricted to a still small number of respondents (14.81%). In contrast, rates of participation of the beneficiaries in the village affairs and party affairs are 90% and 23% respectively. In other words, the extent of participation of the beneficiaries is higher than that of the non-beneficiaries in both diffuse and specific categories, as shown in Table 6.14.

Table 6.14
Comparing the Rates of Political Participation of Beneficiaries and Non-beneficiaries Based on Political Inclination

Type of Participation	*Beneficiaries (% out of 130)*	*Non-beneficiaries (% out of 65)*
Diffuse	90	51.8
Specific	23	14.81

The comparison of political preferences of the two groups shows that at the state level, the congress government is preferred by 37.69% of the beneficiary respondents and 25.92% of the non-beneficiary respondents. However, a greater percentage of non-beneficiaries (26%) prefer Janata Dal Government which has the backing of 16.92% of the beneficiaries. 8.4% of beneficiaries and 7.34% of the non-beneficiaries are critical of a Congress Government as well as a Janata Dal Government. Those who express their incapacity to exercise their choice in the matter constitute 36.92% of the beneficiaries and 40.74% of the non-beneficiaries. The following table shows the political preference of the beneficiaries and the non-beneficiaries at the state level:

Table 6.15
Political Preference of the Beneficiaries and Non-beneficiaries at the State Level

Categories of Preference	*Beneficiaries (% out of 130)*	*Non-beneficiaries (% out of 65)*
Want a Congress government	37.69	25.92
Want a Janata government	16.92	26.00
Want neither Congress nor Janata	8.46	7.34
Can't say	36.92	40.77
Total	99.99	100.00

At the Centre, the preference of the beneficiaries for a Congress-led Government (28.46%) compares favourably with the similar preference of non-beneficiaries (29.6%). A small percentage of the beneficiaries (6.15%) favour ot Janata Dal Government while none of the non-beneficiaries is inclined towards a Janata Dal government at the centre. The percentages of respondents among the beneficiaries and non-beneficiaries who are cynical of both the Congress and the Janata Dal ruling at the centre are 11.53 and 7.4 respectively. The respondents who could not exercise their preference about this have a share of 53.88% among the beneficiaries and 63% among the non-beneficiaries. The following table shows the comparative political preference of the beneficiaries and the non-beneficiaries about the party to rule at the centre:

Table 6.16
Political Preference of the Beneficiaries and the Non-beneficiaries About the Centre

Categories of Preference	*Beneficiaries (% out of 130)*	*Non-beneficiaries (% out of 65)*
Want a Congress Govt.	28.46	29.6
Want of Janata Dal Led govt.	6.15	NIL
Want neither Congress nor Janata	11.53	7.4
Can't Say	53.88	63
Total	100.00	100.00

Based on the figures given in the two Tables 15 and 16, we can derive the rates of the critical participation of both the groups of tribals at the state and national levels based on their relative political preference for a certain type of government.

Table 6.17
Critical Participation of Beneficiaries and Non-beneficiaries at State and National Levels

Level of Critical Participation	*Beneficiaries (% out of 1330)*	*Non-beneficiaries (% out of 65)*
Centre	15.37	12.3
State	21.02	19.75

The comparison of the critical participation of the two groups of tribals shows that the beneficiaries have a higher rate of critical participation than the non-beneficiaries, both at the centre and in the state.

The participation of the non-beneficiaries in the local politics in terms of the frequency of their attendance in political meetings shows a few trends. Like the beneficiaries, the non-beneficiaries take great interest in Gram Sabha and those who abstain from its meetings constitute only 18.5% of the respondents. We find a negative trend among both the tribal groups in the matter of attendance in Gram Panchayat meetings as evident from a very high degree of abstention in such meetings among the beneficiaries (87.69%) as well as non-beneficiaries (88.88%). However, non-beneficiaries show a higher degree of involvement in attending Gram Sabha meetings always (40%) vis-a-vis the beneficiaries whose attendance frequency in this respect is 35.38%. Among the beneficiary respondents who attend Gram sabha meetings sometimes constitute 41.53% which is greater than attendance frequency of the non-beneficiaries (33.33%) in this respect. The frequency of non-beneficiaries attendance in Gram Panchayat meetings is higher (11.11%) compared to attendance rate of beneficiaries (7.69%). All in all, the non-beneficiaries score better as far as regular attendance in Gram Sabha meetings is concerned. The regular attendance of the beneficiaries in Gram Panchayata meetings, however, is better compared to that of the non-beneficiaries. The occasional attendance of the beneficiaries is higher in the gram sabha meetings while non-beneficiaries have a higher rate of regular attendance in Gram Panchayat meetings. However, it is apparent that there is no significant difference between the two groups in respect of grass-roots participation.

Table 6.18

Showing the Extent of Grass Roots Participation of the Non-beneficiaries in Term of Frequency of Attendance in Gram Sabha and Gram Panchayat Meetings

Attendance Frequency	*Non-beneficiaries attending Gram Sabha meetings (% out of 65)*	*Non-beneficiaries attending Gram Panchayat meetings (% out of 65)*
Always	40	NIL
Sometimes	33.33	11.11
Rarely	7.4	NIL
Noneat all	18.5	88.88
Total	99.23	99.99

In both categories, the percentage of those who do not attend the meetings of Gram Panchayat at all is very high while a substantial majority of members in both groups attend the meetings of the Gram Sabha. This is perhaps due to the fact that they regard the Gram Sabha as a part of village life while the Gram Panchayat is perceived by them as an alien body involving a lot of complexities. This shows that the gram panchayat has not yet been able to capture the mind and imagination of the tribals.

Looking at the extent of effective political participation, we have observed that the village level redressal in case of the non-beneficiaries is confined exclusively to the level of local political leaders such as ward members, sarpanch etc. and extends to 25.76% of the respondents. Unlike the beneficiaries, they do not approach the village elders with their grievances. The overall rate of participation of the tribal beneficiaries (63%) at the village level is much higher than that of the non-beneficiaries. Like the beneficiaries, non-beneficiaries rarely approach the M.L.A. or the M.P. While redressal at the police level is confined to 7.4% of the respondents among the non-beneficiaries, we, do not have a single instance of redressal at this level, in case of beneficiaries. Tribals, whether beneficiaries or non-beneficiaries, maintain a safe distance from law courts in the matter of grievance redressal. The rate of official level redressal is at par covering 15% in both categories. The non-beneficiaries who can not think of redressal of any kind constitute a greater percentage (48.14%) compared to the beneficiaries in this respect (15.52%). However, taken as a whole, non-beneficiaries participate more effectively in redressing their grievances at the system level comprising the officials, courts and the police compared to the beneficiaries seeking redressal at this/these levels. The following table shows the patterns of grievance redressal in case of the non-beneficiaries:

Table 6.19
Rate of Non-beneficiary Participation on the Basis of Grievance Redressal

Level of Grievance	*Non-Beneficiaries (%)*
Village elders	NIL
Local political leaders	25.76
M.L.A.	NIL
M.P.	3.7
Police	7.4
Courts	NIL
Officials	15
Non-redressal	48.14
Total	100.00

The rate of effective participation of the non-beneficiaries at the system level which includes the three levels of the police, the courts and the officials is 22.4%. In the case of beneficiaries, the rate of effective political participation is 15.38%, as we have seen earlier. The difference in the rates of effective participation of the two groups is due to the fact that the beneficiaries take into consideration the officials only for their grievance redressal while the non-beneficiaries consider approaching officials as well as the police for the purpose. At the official level alone, however, there is hardly any difference in the participation of the two groups.

Political awareness survey among the non-beneficiaries reveal that they have greater awareness of national politics compared to the beneficiaries. 11% of the non-beneficiaries have heard of our constitution, 18.5% know about the President of India, 37% have information about the local MP's visit to the area and a huge majority of 92.59% realise the usefulness of the Photo-Identify Card. Acquaintance with the M.L.A. or his contribution is not considered as important as in the case of beneficiaries. 55% of the respondents among the non-beneficiaries are familiar with the local M.L.A. and about 25% of them know about his contribution. Regarding information on local politics, tribals in both categories have about the same degree of awareness. 96% of the non-beneficiaries are familiar with the Sarpanch and 30% have some knowledge of the G.P., its activities and the sources of funding etc.

Our study of political perception of the non-beneficiaries shows that 74% of them are non-political in nature. 4% of the non-beneficiaries view politics as a vocation and thus belong to the professional category while 3.7% of them follow the commands of the village bosses and belong to the "Ram" type, A communitarian attitude towards politics is observed in case of 7.4% of the non-beneficiary respondents. Those who like to treat politics as a means of promoting common welfare constitute 11.11% and thus belong to the ideal category. There is none in the cynical category. The machiavellian type too is absent among the non-beneficiaries. The following 3D pie-diagram shows the percentage distribution of the non-beneficiaries among the eight types of "political men" which we have enlisted.

CONCLUDING OBSERVATIONS

The above statistics may give rise to the following inferences. One, the beneficiaries having availed themselves

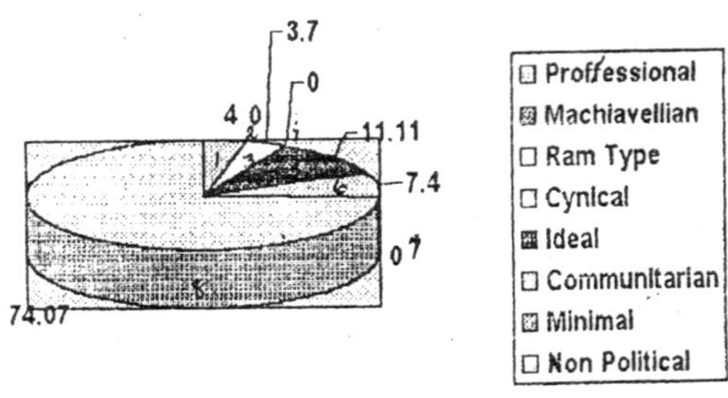

Non-Beneficiary Typology Based on Political Perception

of developmental benefits have been able to significantly improve their socio-economic condition. As compared to non-beneficiaries, the awareness and political interest of the beneficiaries have increased. Because of their frequent interaction with local leaders as well as developmental officials, they have gained in self-confidence. The cumulative effect of these processes has been a marked rise in the participation of the beneficiaries. Moreover, they may also have been motivated by the consideration that such participation will bring them more of benefits from the government. Development process may not only have resulted in greater well being and better participation of the tribals but it may also have brought about a change in their attitude and perception. Our study of the political perceptions of the beneficiaries and non-beneficiaries reveals the truth of the observation. According to the findings, compared to the non-beneficiaries, the beneficiaries are less apathetic, more realistic and more politically inclined.

REFERENCES

1. L. Milbrath, *Political Participation* (Chicago, R. and McNally, 1985).
2. See S.M. Lipset, *Political Man* (New Delhi, Arnold-Heinemann India, 1973).
3. See For a critical and empathetic discussion of the new developments arising out of Kandha-Pana conflict, see B.N. Mohapatra and D. Bhattacharya, "Tribal-Dalit Conflict-Electoral Politics in Phulbani", *Economic and Political Weekly,* Mumbai. January 13–20. 1996, pp. 160-164).
4. See Bruce M. Russet and Others, *World Handbook of Political and Social Indicators* (New Haven, Conn., 1964), pp. 293-303 for a classification of societies.
5. See Robert Lane, *Political Life: Why people get involved in politics* (Glencoe Illinois, 1959), pp. 102 and 104.
6. See S.M. Lipset. *Political Man* (New Delhi. Arnold-Heinemann India, 1973).

7. See Human Development Report 1993. Published for the United Nations Development Programme (New York, Oxford University Press, 1993), pp. 21.
8. *Ibid.*
9. S.M. Lipset defines effective participation as the extent to which the system (administrative and legal) satisfies the basic functions of the Government in the opinion of the people.

7

SUMMARY AND CONCLUSION

SOCIAL MATRIX OF POVERTY AND DEVELOPMENT

The process of rural development in India has been largely exogenous in nature involving the use of an alien governmental apparatus, application of technological innovations and provisions of institutional finance. In contrast, culture is woven around age-old beliefs and practices of people and therefore, *sui generis,* in nature. Poverty which constitutes the bed rock of such a culture has a overriding socio-spatial dimension, although it is essentially an economic phenomenon. It is an integral component of the collective consciousness of people fostered by religion from times immemorial. Religiousity of the Hindus have made them insensitive to the material advancement in different parts of the world. They have accepted and absorbed alien influences without being sensitised to the promise of a better worldly life. Commenting on Hindu conservatism, Nirad C. Choudhury writes, "the rigidity (of Hindu culture increased through the ages as the danger to the identity continued and grew). The Muslims had used force, the English had held out temptation and that was a greater peril... as nationalism grew under British rule, so did the religious conservatism..... Thus it may be said that from the Aryan self-consciousness to the recent Hindu self-consciousness, there is an unbroken line of descent"[1].

This collective self consciousness is what makes the Indian society unitarian, rigid and less amenable to change. Therefore, to force a non-material society to develop along the material lines is to shake the foundations of that society rudely. Further, all developments, in the ultimate analysis, are social, if not religious in character.

Village constitutes the arena for the developmental experiments. It is here too, where Hindu society and culture lives strongly and merrily in the midst of poverty. Interventions into village life are viewed as necessarily authoritarian, alien and destructive of the social fabric and use of the state machinery for development even on egalitarian lines, is not only banal but also anti-society and anti-people.

The attack on poverty has in effect meant an attack on society which is stratified and poverty-sustaining, by bringing the structure of society rooted in religious values and culture norms under role structures of modernity. Caste has in the process under gone radical transformation of roles, developed new functional adaptations and activated aspirations unleased by democratisation of polity and power structure .... Now it functions as an important structure network in the process of modernisation.[2] Gunnar Myrdal[3] supports a radical departure from the value systems of the developing society as a prelude to growth of modern instrumental structures viz. income, production etc. Sociologists[4], on the other hand, view such radical changes as fatal to the social structure, especially in India where democratic polity and way of life have been accepted as independent values. They make a plea for a democratic form of modernisation, making room for institutional coordination of modernising changes, so that the social costs of development are kept within tolerable limits.

Development has generally been considered as a surface reality, assessing its performance in terms of success and failure. Some have attributed the failures of programmes to lapses in implementation, while others have found fault in the strategy. Some experts have recommended 'mid-course' corrections to rectify the lapses during implementation. The critics who attribute the development failures to centralised planning advocate the adoption and popularisation of the participative approach for better results. But very few have questioned the ideology of development which, according to some critics, represents a systematic onslaught of world capitalism against the economically-weak nations and an attempt to convert cultures into territories of the international capitalist market. No price is considered big enough for world hegemony by the international capitalists. It is a subtle process achieved through the creation of artificial growth-needs by whetting up aspirations and taking prompt steps to ensure meeting of those needs by the people. The entire communication network such as television, newspapers—is vigorously used to propagate growth and development in terms of restructured needs using western symbols and images. In this sense, there is a cultural strategy to spread the ideology of market capitalism.

Irrespective of its ideological undertones, development has come to be accepted as the credo of the times. People living in the rural areas, especially the tribals and other socially and economically weaker sections of mankind, however ironical it may seem, have to keep pace with time in order that they survive and grow. Admittedly, there are casualties inflicted in the process. Enlightened opinion in this regard is in favour of adapting to the demands of modernisation while keeping the social costs and casualties which accompany the development process to the minimum.

In this thesis, we have examined the operational dimensions of development in a tribal Gram Panchayat in the context of political participation and its consequences for the soceity. On the basis of our finding, we have made certain generalisations about the impact of development on the tribe and the tribal political participation.

FINDINGS OF THE STUDY

Finding No. 1: In the present study, an attempt has been made to establish a positive correlation between accretion of developmental benefits to the tribals and a rise in their standard of living. We have compared the annual per capita family income of the beneficiaries with that of the non-beneficiaries and found that the former are better off economically than the latter. 12.3% of the respondents among beneficiaries are found to be above the poverty line while non-beneficiaries enjoying the similar economic status constitute only 3.7%. Further, one finds that the presence of the very poor among the beneficiaries is quite sizeable (46.16%), yet smaller in comparison to their presence among the non beneficiaries (55.55%). However, the percentage of the poor and the poorest in the ranks of the beneficiaries and non-beneficiaries is just about the same. The above comparison vindicates our first hypothesis. The benefits of development accruing to the tribals have contributed to a better standard of living.

From the standpoint of consumption also the above hypothesis stands vindicated. A comparison of data regarding the annual family per capita consumption expenditure of the beneficiaries and non-beneficiaries shows that only 52.30% of the beneficiaries spend up to Rs. 10,000 per annum while, this minimal upper limit applies to a vast majority non-beneficiaries (88.88%), Beneficiaries with an annual expenditure upto Rs, 20,000 constitute 44.61% while the same volume of annual expenditure is afforded by only 11.11% of the non-beneficiaries. The uppermost expenditure limit is afforded by 3.07% of the beneficiaries while there is not a single non-beneficiary who can spend so much.

Thus we reach the conclusion that the process of development has resulted in a much better standard of living for the beneficiaries both in terms of higher income and expenditure levels, compared to the non-beneficiaries.

Finding No. 2 : Our study of the impact of the process of development on the occupational structure suggest two trends: (i) the implementation of developmental programmes has encouraged the beneficiaries to take up occupations different from the ones they were engaged earlier. In other words, it has made them occupationally mobile. (ii) It has also encouraged some of them to take up a second occupation in addition to the existing one, as a supplementary source of income leading to occupational diversification.

The first trend is indicated by the acceptance of the daily wage work by the tribals of Phulbani district in ever greater frequency, leaving their customary occupations. An Indian sociologist Late Prof. B.K. Nanda[5] testifies to the trend in his study of the *Bonda* tribe of the Koraput district of highland Orissa. According to him, wage labour or contractual labour is the new economic frontier which is constantly expanding while *Odja* labour or cooperative labour prevalent among them is declining.

The popularity of wage labour known also as *buti* is due to the fact that it ensures ready remuneration and that it is free from customary obligation. While *Odja* upholds the supremacy of the clan, *buti* establishes the primacy of the state. We notice a similar trend in the case of the *Kandha* tribe of the Phulbani district where the new paradigm of work has come to stay at the expense of the old one, the paradigm of 'vernacular work'.[6]

Our study has revealed that 72.1% of the beneficiaries are engaged in a single occupation which is less than the percentage of non-beneficiaries (81.4%) thus engaged. Beneficiaries who are engaged in more than one occupation constitute 22.52% which is more than twice the number of non-beneficiaries (11.1%) with a mixture of occupations. In the category of daily wage labour alone, 18.4% the beneficiaries are there which is less than the share of non-beneficiaries (22.2%). Among the beneficiaries, some of the farmers and petty businessmen using daily wage labour as second source of income constitute two of the mixed categories with a combined share of 5.3%. Beneficiaries combining business with service (1.5%) constitute the third mixed category. The emergence of the mixed categories is a pointer to the second trend, that of occupational diversification.

The data presented above prove that the process of development has not only contributed to occupational mobility by offering alternative work opportunities but also accounts for gradual diversification of the occupational structure.

Finding No. 3 : The study also finds out that the impact of development on the levels of awareness and activity of the tribals has been rather positive. The beneficiaries display a much better awareness with regard to state politics compared to the non-beneficiaries as a result of their direct or indirect involvement in the activities related to procurement of development assistance which includes not only a knowledge of various formalities at various official levels but also a host of activities such as interactions with officials in charge of supervising these activities. Tribals awareness about and participation in local political institutions and affairs has been found to be fairly good which may be due to the fact that, for most of the development related activities, the local institutions function as the intermediary level acting as a bridge between the beneficiaries and the block, district level officials. Since the national level politics is of no direct consequence to the beneficiaries, it is not expected to feature high in their agenda.

Our analysis, however, reveals that developmental participation has generally led to an increase of awareness and activities of beneficiaries. However, it may be mentioned here that greater participation by the beneficiaries may not necessarily be the consequence of literacy as there is no significant difference between the literacy levels of the beneficiaries and non-beneficiaries. The literacy level of the beneficiaries of the Alami GP is in any case, reasonably high (53.08%) and that of the non-beneficiaries is 51.86%, the former being marginally higher than the latter.

Finding No. 4 : The study then goes on to test the hypothesis about the implications of development for social and political participation of tribals. It has been found that developmental activities have stimulated social and political participation. Let us take up the case of social participation. First, the rate of participation in village affairs among tribals is as high as 90% while the rate of village level redressal which is another form of social participation is 63%. The rate of participation of tribal non-beneficiaries in these two types of activities are 51.8% and 25.76% respectively which are much less than the rate of beneficiary participation.

As far as political participation is concerned we can cite a number of examples to prove our hypothesis. To begin with, membership of political parties, the beneficiaries have shown higher degree of involvement (23%) compared to the non-beneficiaries (14.81%). As far as electoral participation is concerned, both the groups are almost on the same level. But in the allied electoral activities, the participation of beneficiaries is way ahead of non-beneficiaries. The relatively higher degree of social and political participation of tribals can logically be attributed to benefits procured under various development schemes.

Finding No. 5 : Political participation may lead to several socio-political changes. We have sought to assess the impact of participation on the traditional power structure, employing an indirect method of analysis. The study of trends in local political participation has shown that the Gram Sabha is immensely popular among tribals, beneficiaries as well as non-beneficiaries.

While there is a variation in the response of the two groups with regard to the Gram Panchayat meetings, the regular participation of the beneficiaries in such meetings is no doubt, not very high (3.07%) but still it is a key factor in the decision-making process at the local level. There is a complete absence of such participation among the non-beneficiaries. It may be deduced that a small section of the tribals who have been assisted is beginning to feel the importance of the representative political leaders at the grass-root level.

Besides, beneficiaries have higher rate of occasional attendance at the Gram Sabha meeting compared to the non-beneficiaries which shows that the former prefer to attend these meetings selectively and that their participation is issue-based. This speaks of the ability of a greater number of beneficiaries to discriminate between important and unimportant meetings. Indiscriminate attendance indirectly amounts to legitimizing the social authority of a new village bosses who conduct such meetings.

From the above, we get an indication that beneficiaries are a little ahead of the non-beneficiaries in discovering the new source of authority, which more than one-tenth in both the groups of tribals constituting a sizeable segment of the tribal population share the new perspective.

Furthermore, local participation in developmental activities has shown that people are ready to change their earlier occupation in favour of daily wage labour or contractual wage labour known as *buti*. The emergence of wage economy involving ready payment of wage at rates fixed by the state implies the acceptance of the supremacy of the secular authority and gradual rejection of social authority (authority of the clan). The attachment to a traditional occupation implies unquestioned acceptance of the social power structure in the form of the owner-worker bond which is absent in the daily wage work.

Findings No. 6 : Development induces social and political participation, as we have already seen. Likewise, political participation creates an environment for modernisation. It generates a feeling of confidence among the tribals. The community prepares itself for developmental interventions at a psychological plane. Participation breaks social isolation of the tribals and paves the way for individual welfare as well as community development. It encourages them to increase their awareness and activities. The community yearns for education, civic amenities, irrigation, electricity, transport, communication and learns to convert these wants into demands and seeks their fulfilment through their representative political leaders. The 'closed moral community' of the tribals is helped to open up slowly and gradually through majority participation in various political activities. The need structure and the aspiration level of the members of a tribal community which had been defined for years are seen to be changing as a consequence of political participation.

Political participation facilitates integration of tribals into the mainstream in several ways: (i) by providing opportunities for self development, (ii) by tuning their life style along modern lines, (iii) by encouraging them to speak for themselves and their community, (iv) by allowing them the means to restructure their society, (v) by creating a progressive leadership which is less committed to the clan and more commited to the State/Nation.

In practical terms, the institutions of the state, at the block, tehsil and district levels have become the alternative centres of reference/authority for the tribals. Participation in the assembly and parliamentary elections equip them for much bigger roles in the society. In spite of low literacy level and poor communication, they attend political meetings in good number. Some canvass during the elections on behalf of the political parties while a few jump into the election fray as candidates sharing a party platform. Besides, they rarely fail to cast their votes. All these point to a attitudinal change which is conducive for modernisation.

Finding No. 7: Another consequence of political participation is that, it produces capacities for group organisation, and thus, social groups vying for power and identity. It creates new kinds of group loyalties, for the tribal people transcending the kinship and locality barier. It helps them to develop political choices of their own, identify new goals and priorities and enables them to explore new frontiers of identity. It provides them, with the scope to integrate the role of citizen with that of a society man. It prepares them for leadership roles too.

Participation in the activities of the fora such as youth clubs, Mahila Samities facilitates articulation of group feelings. The legal protection for participatory activities of socially weaker groups for power sharing comes in the form of constitutional provision for reservation of seats in representatives bodies at the local level. Active involvement in activities such as canvassing, organizing and attending political meetings produces among tribals new capacities of management and organisation of human affairs and resources. In contesting elections, one is seen as representing a particular group from which he comes and thus becomes a symbol of identity and power for that group. In short political participation, equips them to take part in the game of power as leaders of particular interest groups.

In this regard, the introduction of the tribals into the constituency politics is of particular importance, as it has unleashed new possibilities. As Prof. F.G. Bailey[7] has pointed out, constituency is an arena of political mobilization linking two other socio-political arenas of political mobilisation—village and elite. Besides, it largely determines the form and character of the linkages between the two. With the passage of time, the tribals have developed preferences identifying themselves with key political organisations operating at this level.

Finding No. 8: A corollary of the above function is: political participation increases bargaining power of tribals vis-a-vis other social groups and vis-a-vis the state. Prof. Bailey has referred to this aspect of social relations and power against the backdrop of 1957 Assembly elections where political choices were determined by the rising assertion of *Panas* against the Khandayats of Bisipara Village.[8] But it was largely a matter confined to the village. In the 1995 Assembly elections, on the contrary, the political choices were determined by the tribe-caste conflict *(Kandhas* versus *Panas*) which preceded it. And there was political mobilisation not merely in the village where the conflict first germinated, but it encompassed the members of the two communities living in the nook and corner of the district and the impact of such mobilisation was nation-wide. Out of such mobilisation, a new political platform, the Kandhamal Vikas Parishad (KVP) was born. This was not only an act of political assertion by a culturally homogenous group. It was much more than that. The new platform symbolised the tribals' distrust of the dominant political parties (Congress and Janata Dal) as far as safeguarding the interest of the tribal community was concerned. It was also a protest against the politics of appeasement of these parties by the tribals, whose identity as a community came under serious threat.

In the 1995, Assembly polls, KVP set up its own candidate with the traditional community symbol of bow and arrow, collected its won election fund from the members of the community and issued a radical character of demands. For the first time since the first General Election, an indigenous political organisation was successful in ousting the major national and regional parties from the local electoral arena.

The win of the KVP candidate represented the victory of the tribals vis-a-vis the *Panas* on the one hand vis-a-vis the state on the other.

The incidences signified the revolutionary potentials of political participation such as increase in the level of political mobilisation and consequently, the bargaining power of social groups *vis-a-vis* the state.

Finding No. 9: Political participation brings about a change in the elite profile. As we have noted above, elite represents one of the three arenas of political mobilisation susceptible to change. Election of representative leaders at the Gram Panchayat level/Panchayat Samiti level representing the newly formed interest groups is facilitated through political participation resulting in a departure from the earlier composition in these bodies usually comprising the dominant and vested social interests. Further, participation has facilitated the entry of more and more women, as a result of 30% reservation of seats in the local representative bodies. However, the change in the elite profile is a slow process in the tribal community as the social hierarchy which throws up political leadership at the local levels, continues to be powerful, though much weaker compared to the past.

The impetus for development must come from within the village and from within the community. Development process should be accelerated partly through local initiative which a progressive local leadership with its eyes on popularity and power is capable of providing. It is through this leadership that the prerequisite conditions for development can be created at the village level. The initiatives include adopting new technologies to accommodate new patterns of trade, business and vocations, providing broad based institutional credit mechanism in the accessible areas, providing facilities of transport and communication for marketing the surplus etc.

The constituency level leadership of course has a far greater role as far as representing the community interest, in the state and national fora is concerned. Since national political parties have now spread far and wide in the tribal district, the involvement of tribals in party activities has given rise to political pressure groups among tribals. While the social dominance of village bosses is reflected in the composition of local political institutions, it is considerably weaker in the sphere of state and national politics. The constituency sphere is being utilised by the tribals who are more exposed and more dynamic rather than those who are socially entrenched and traditionally dominant.

Finding No. 10: There is also a negative mode of political participation which results from the gradual marginalisation of certain sections of the society. We have found in this study that those tribals who have been deprived of development assistance because of administrative lapses have participated in airing their grievances at various level—village levels, political level, system level etc.

The study reveals that the participation of the non-beneficiaries is higher compared to the beneficiaries as far as redressal of grievances at the system level is concerned. In other words, the participation of the deprived tribals is more effective than the beneficiaries, as indicated by a higher degree of political mobilisation in case of the former (20.4%) *vis-a-vis* that of the latter (15.38%). The finding testifies to the last of our hypothesis: Deprivation from development benefits instead of leading to indifference and non-participation, leads to political mobilisation in the form of protest.

DEVELOPMENT, DEMOCRACY AND TRANSITION

The fissures in tribal society are beginning to surface under the combined impact of development and political participation. The isolation of the tribals which their culture cosmology and the rigid social structure have fostered for long years is being replaced through their adaptation and accommodation into the secular mainstream of the nation. The extent to which the process of change can continue with the traditional aspects of society is a matter of conjecture.

The development experiments in the recent years, have brought to our notice the severe stress in tribal life and their cultural identity is said to be the worst casualty of development. The subjectivity of the *Kandhas* is deeply embedded in an animistic religion and culturally prescribed rituals which account for their social solidarity. This solidarity is in turn, responsible for collective subjugation of tribals vis-a-vis the secular society. It has endowed them with a wholesome and homogenous community life. At the same time, it has limited their mental horizon. The tribals find themselves precariously caught between the conflicting demands of being and becoming.

Living on the ground as they do, the tribals can not know what future holds for them—A view from above will always tell us better about how the groundsmen are doing. This is precisely the view of the developmentalists who operate from above having the advantages of knowledge and location which the tribals lack so conspicuously. It is this contrast between the native's ground level 'feel' and the gladiator's top down 'view' which is epitomised in the clash between culture and development.

The theory that tribals know best as to what is good for them is microscopic, though anthropomorphic. On the contrary, the developmentalists' impatience with the tribal 'lethargy' to catch up with time smacks of their colonising intention. The 'subject' should not be reduced to the level of an object. At the same time, the subject must be encouraged to transcend his subjectivity in order that he may acquire a new one to suit the requirements of time.

It. is appropriate to place political participation somewhere in the transitional process as playing the role of reconciliation, along with education. As our study has revealed political participation prepares a climate for modernisation. In an exclusive context of tribal culture, no meaningful economic and political participation, is possible. Tribals must be motivated to change their outlook and an willingness to accept change must be inculcated into them. The locus of development is anything but culture. Creation of a new centre or locus is a slow and painful process. The perception of life is bound to change as new opportunities start flowing in and as there is a shift of paradigm.

It will be foolish to say that the tribals are a contented lot and they do not aspire for a better life. But it must be borne in mine that they must be helped first to transcend their identity barrier so that they start treating themselves as an economically disadvantaged section of the population rather than a cultural group. This will facilitate decentering which is a prerequisite for their economic development and indicates a shift from the realm of sprit to the realm of matter.

REFERENCES

1. For a Critical discussion on Hinduism. See Nirad Choudhury, *Hinduism,* 1967.
2. See Yogendra Singh, *Modenisation of Indian Tradition* (New Delhi, Manohar 1979).
3. See Gunnar Myrdal, *The Asian Drama—An Inqviry into the Poverty of Nations* (London, Allen Lane: The Fenguin, 1968).
4. *Op. cit.* 68.
5. See Bikram Narayan Nanda, "Venacular Work, Wage Labour and Tribal Development: A Case Study of Highland Orissa", *Contributions to India Sociology* (New Delhi), January-June 1992, pp. 115–132.

6. The term "vernacular work" has been introduced by Ivan Illich.
7. F.G. Bailey, *Politics and Social Change—Orissa in 1959* (Berkeley, University of California, 1963).
8. *Ibid.*

BIBLIOGRAPHY

BOOKS

A.K. Danda, *Tribal Economics and Their Transformations* (New Delhi, Indian Council of Social Science Research, 1973).

A.R. Basu, *Tribal Development Programmes and Administration in India* (New Delhi, National Book Organisation, 1985).

A.R. Desai, *Changing Profile of Rural India and Human Rights of the Agrarian Poor; An Assessment of Strategy of Rural Development since Independence* (Chandigarh, CRRID Publication, 1990).

A.R. Desai, *The Scheduled Tribes* (Mumbai, Popular, 1963).

A.V. Rama Rao, *Evaluation of Integrated Tribal Development Agency, Khammam District, Andhra Pradesh* (Hyderabad, the Indian Institute of Economics, 1982).

Akhter Ahmed Khan, *Collected Works : 3 vols* (Camilla, Bangladesh Academy of Rural Development, 1983).

Amal Ray and Vanita Vehkatasubbaiah, *Studies in Rural Development Administration* (Calcutta, World Press, 1984).

Arun Majumdar, *Poverty, Development and Exchange Relations — A Study of two Birbhum Villages* (New Delhi, Radiant, 1987).

Arvind N. Das, *India Invented—A Nation-in-the Making* (New Delhi, Manohar, 1994).

Ashwani Saith, *Development Strategies and the Rural Poor* (Geneva, International Labour Organisation, 1989).

Azizar Rahman Khan & Eddy Lee, *Poverty Asia, Rural Bangkok* (Geneva, International Labour Organisation, 1984).

B. Das and Others. *Planning and Regional Planning— Concepts and Case Studies in Orissa* (Berhampur: Orissa. Berhampur University, 1978).

B.C. Mehta, *Rural Poverty in India* (New Delhi, Concept, 1993).

B.K. Roy Burman, *Towards Poverty Alleviation Programmes in Nagaland and Manipur* (Delhi, Mittal Publications, 1984).

B.N. Sahay, *Pragmatism in Development: Application of Anthropology* (New Delhi, Book Hive, 1969).

Bernard Van Heck, *Participation of Poor in Rural Organisation* (Rome, Food and Agriculture Organisation, 1979).

Bimal Jalan, *India's Economic Policy : Preparing for the Twenty-First Century* (New Delhi, Viking, 1996).

Binoy N. Verma and Birendra Prasad, *IRDP : The Vision Reality Gap* (New Delhi, Eastern Books, 1991).

Bipin Behari, *Rural Poverty and Center Unemployment* (New Delhi, Vikas Publishing House, 1990).

Bruce M. Russet and others, *World Handbook of Political and Social Indicators* (New Haven, Conn., 1964).

C.B. Mamoria, *Tribal Demography of India* (Allahabad, Kitab Mahal, 1957).

C.H.H. Rao, *Technological Change and Distribution of Gains in Indian Agriculture* (New Delhi, MacMillan, 1975).

C.P. Bhambri, *Politics in India : 1947–1987* (New Delhi, Vikas, 1988). Chris Dixon, *Rural Development in the Third World* (London, Routledge, 1990).

Clifford Geertz, *Old Societies and New States* (Illinois, Glencoe, 1963).

D. Hardiman, *The Coming of the Devi: Adivasis in Western India* (New Delhi, Oxford University Press, 1982).

D. Spencer Hatch, *Further Upward in Rural India* (London, Oxford University Press, 1938).

D.G. Mandelbaum, *Society in India* (Mumbai, Popular, 1970).

D.M. Praharaj, *Tribal Movements and Political History in India* (New Delhi, Inter India, 1988).

D.S. Nag, *Tribal Economy : An Economic Study of Baiga* (Delhi, Bharatiya Adimjati Sevak Sangh, 1958).

D.V. Raghava Rao, *Panchayats and Rural Development Studies in Integrated Rural Development* (New Delhi, Ashish, 1980).

David Brokensha and Peter Hodge, *Community Development—An Interpretation* (San Francisco, Chandler, 1969).

David E. Apter, *Political Change* (London, Frank Cass. 1973).

Devendra Thakur, *Rural Development and Planning in India* (New Delhi, Deep and Deep, 1989).

Douglas Ensminger, *Rural India in Transition* (New Delhi, All India Panchayat Parishad, 1972).

Durganand Sinha, *Indian Villages in Transition—A Motivational Analysis* (New Delhi, Associated Publishing House, 1969).

Earl M. Kulp, *Rural Development Planning: Systems Analysis and Working Method* (New York, Praeger, 1970).

Elliot R. Morris etc., *Strategies For Small Farmer Development—African Cases* (Boulder, West View Press, 1976).

F. Tummason Jannuzi, *Agrarian Crisis in India—The case of Bihar* (Mumbai, Sangam, 1974).

F.G. Bailey, *Caste and Economic Frontier* (Mumbai, Oxford University Press, 1958).

F.G. Bailey, *Politics and Social Change—Orissa in 1959* (Berkeley, University of California, 1963).

F.G. Bailey, *Tribe, Caste and Nation* (Manchester, Manchester University Press, 1960).

F.L. Brayne, *Village Uplift in India* (Allahabad, Pioneer Press, 1927).

Florence R. Kluckhon and Fred L. Stordtbeck, *Variation In Value—Orientation Row* (New York, Patterson and Company, 1961).

Food and Agriculture Organisation, *Agrarian Reform and Rural Development* (Rome, FAO, 1979).

Francine R, Frankel, *India's Green Revolution—Economic Gains and Political Costs* (Princeton, Princeton University, 1971).

Francine, R. Frankel, *India's Political Economy:* 1947–1977—The Gradual Revolution (Delhi, Oxford University Press, 1978).

Franz Fanon, *The Wretched of the Earth* (London, Penguin, 1967).

G. Almond and S. Verba, *The Civic Culture* (Illinois, Glencoe, 1959).

G. Hargopal, *Administrative Leadership and Rural Development in India* (New Delhi, Light and Life Publishers, 1980).

G.E. Sussman, *The Challenge of Integrated Rural Development in India* (Colorado, Westview Press, 1982).

G.K. Lieten, *Continuity and Change in Rural West Bengal* (New Delhi, Sage, 1992).

G.R. Madan and Tara Madan, *Village Development in India—A Sociological Approach* (New Delhi, Allied, 1983).

G.R. Madan, *India's Developing Villages* (Lucknow, Printhouse, 1983).

G.S. Ghurye, *The Aboriginals So-called and Their Future* (Pune, Gokhale Institute, 1943).

G.S. Ghurye, *The Scheduled Tribes* (Mumbai, Popular, 1963).

G.V.K. Rao, *Existing administrative Arrangements for Rural Development and Poverty Alleviation Programmes* (New Delhi, Department of Rural Development: Government of India, 1985).

G.V.S. DeSilva and Others, *Towards a Theory of Rural Development* (Lahore, Progressive Publishers, 1988).

George F. Gant, *Development Administration: Concepts, Goal, Methods* (Wisconsin, University of Wisconsin, 1979).

Gerry Rogers, *Population Growth and Poverty in Rural Asia* (New Delhi, Sage, 1989).

Ghanashyam Shah, *Economic Differentiation and Tribal Identity* (Delhi, Ajanta, 1984).

Gilbert Etienne, *Food and Poverty : India's Half-Won Battle* (New Delhi, Sage, 1988).

Gilbert Etienne, *Overall Process of Rural Development-Economic Growth and Social Progress with Special Reference to Asia* (New Delhi, Sage, 1975).

Gilbert Etienne, *Rural Development in Asia—Meetings with Peasants* (New Delhi, Sage, 1985).

Government of India (Planning Commission). *Report of the Programme Evaluation Organisation* (New Delhi, Publication Division, 1957).

Government of India, *Concurrent Evaluation of IRDP: 1985–86* (New Delhi, Ministry of Agriculture/Department of Rural Development, 1986).

Gunnar Myrdal, *The Asian Drama—An Inquiry into the Poverty of Nations* (London, Alien Lane : The Penguin, 1968).

H.S. Verma, *Post-Independence Change in Rural India* (New Delhi, Inter-India, 1980).

Hein Streetkerk and T.K. Moulek, *Managing Rural Development-Health and Energy Programmes in India* (New Delhi, Sage, 1991).

Inderjeet Singh, *The Great Ascent—The Rural Poor in South Asia* (Baltimore, John Hopkins University, 1990).

Indian Institute of Management, *Rural Development for the Rural Poor, Deogarh's Profile* (Ahmedabad, IIM, 1982).

International Labour Organisation, *Profiles of Rural Poverty* (Geneva, ILO, 1979).

Irma Adelman and Sherman Robinsion, *Income Distribution Policies—A Case Study of Korea* (New York, Oxford, 1978).

J. Torisic, *Tribal Religious Beliefs and Practices among the Santals* (New Delhi, Manohar, 1979).

J.B. Ganguly, *Economic—Problem of the Jhumias of Tripura* (Calcutta, Bookland Private Ltd., 1968).

J.C. Jain and Others, *Rural Development Under Government Auspices* (New Delhi, Sage, 1985).

J.C. Kavoori and B.N. Singh, *History of Rural Development in India* (New Delhi, Impex India, 1967).

J.P. Desai and Banwarilal Choudhury, *History of Rural Development in Modem India* (Delhi, IMPEX India, 1977).

J.S. Brar, *Political Economy of Rural Development—Strategies for Poverty Allienation* (New Delhi, Allied, 1983).

J.S. Mathur and others, *Economic and Social Impact of Development Programmes* (Hyderabad, National Institute of Rural Development, 1982).

J.S. Slotkin, *From Field to Factory* (Illinois, Free Press, 1960).

J.S. Sondhi, *Poverty Alleviation and Rural Development* (New Delhi, Criterion, 1990).

James Warner Bjorknan, *Politics of Administrative Alienation in India's Rural Development Programmes* (Delhi, Ajanta, 1979).

Jawaharlal Nehru University, *Statistical Profile of Rural India: District wise* (New Delhi, Centre for Study of Regional Development; JNU, 1977).

John W. Mellor, *Developing Rural India: Plan and Practice* (New Delhi, Sterling, 1979).

Jyotindra Dasgupta, *Authority, Priority and Human Development* (Delhi, Oxford University Press, 1981).

K. Sreenivasan, *Productivity and Social Enviroment* (Mumbai, Asia Publishing House, 1964).

K.A. Raju and others, *Rural Transformation—A Selected Annotated Bibliography of Special Programmes* (Hyderabad, National Institute of Rural Development, 1984).

K.A. Suresh and Joseph Molly, *Cooperatives and Rural Development* (New Delhi, Ashish, 1990).

K.C. Panchanadikar and J. Panchanadikar, *Rural Modernisation in India—A Study in Developmental Infrastructure* (Mumbai, Popular, 1978).

K.M. Bhouraskar, *Tribal Economic Organisation and Market* (Chhindwara, Tribal Research and Training Institute, 1964).

K.R.G. Nair, *Regional Experience in a Developing Economy* (New Delhi, Wiley Eastern, 1982).

K.S. Singh, *Indian Tribes in Transition* (Delhi, Manohar, 1985).

K.S. Singh, *Tribalisation—Tribal Society in India* (New Delhi, Manohar, 1985).

Kailas Sarap, *Development and Change* (New Delhi, Sage, 1990).

Kartar Singh, *Rural Development—Principles, Policies and Management* (New Delhi, Sage, 1986).

Kisan Sharma, *The Konds of Orissa—An Anthropometric Study* (New Delhi, Concept, 1978).

Kuldeep Mathur, *Bureaucratic Response to Development* (Delhi, National, 1972).

L. Milbarth, *Political Participation* (Chicago, Rand McNally, 1985).

L.P. Mathur, *Resistance Movements of Tribals in India* (Udaipur, Himanshu Publications, 1988).

L.S.S. O'Malley, *India's Social Heritage* (New Delhi, Vikas, 1976).

Levy J. Marion, *Modernisation and The Structure of Societies* (Princeton, Princeton University Press, 1966).

Lucian W. Pye, *Politics, Personality and Nation-Building* (New Haven, 1962).

M. Bapuji, *Tribal Development Administration* (Delhi, Kanishka Publishing House, 1993).

M.D. Shalins, *Tribesmen* (New Jeresy, Prentice Hall, 1968).

M. Gluckman, *Close Systems and Open Minds* (Chicago, 1964).

M. Shivlal and Others, *Improving Delivery Systems for Rural Development* (Hyderabad, National Institute of Rural Development, 1985).

M. Sukumaran Nair, *Tribal Economy in Transition: A Study of Meghalaya* (New Delhi, Inter-India Publications, 1987).

M.A. Sherring *Hindu Castes and Tribes — Vol. III* (Delhi, Cosmo Publications, 1974).

M.N. Srinivas, *Caste in Modem India* (Mumbai, Asia Publishing House, 1962).

M.Thaka and Om Prakash, *Integrated Rural Development* (New Delhi, Sterling, 1989).

Madras Institute of Development Studies, *Structure and Intervention—An Evaluation of DPAP, IRDP and Related Programmes in Ramnathpuram and Dharampuri District of Tamilnadu* (Madras, Madras Institute of Development Studies, 1980).

Mahesh Chand and V.K. Puri, *Regional Planning in India* (New Delhi, Allied Publishers Limited, 1983).

Marcus Franda, *Voluntary Association and Local Development in India—The Janata Phase* (New Delhi, Young Asia Publication, 1983).

Max Weber, *The Protestant Ethic and the Spirit of Capitalism* (London, George Allen and Unwin Ltd., 1962).

Mohinder Singh and S.R. Sharma, *Rural Development—A Selected Bibliography* (New Delhi, Uppal Publishing, 1978).

Mohinder Singh, *Rural Development Administration and Anti-Poverty Programmes* (New Delhi, Deep and Deep, 1988).

N. Patnaik, *Tribes and Their Development—A Study of Two Tribal Development Blocks in Orissa* (Hyderabad, National Institute of Community Development, 1972).

National Commission on Agriculture (Government of India), *Report of the National Commission on Agriculture* (New Delhi, Ministry of Agriculture, 1976).

National Institute of Community Development, *Annual Report—1971-72* (Hyderabad, National Institute of Community Development, 1972).

National Institute of Rural Development, *Administrative Arrangement in Rural Development* (Hyderabad, National Institute of Rural Development, 1985).

National Institute of Rural Development, *Rural Development in India—Some Facts* (Hyderabad, N.I.R.D, 1979).

National Institute of Rural Development, *Rural Transformation Regardings* (Hyderabad, N.I.R.D, 1984).

National Institute of Rural Development, *Rural Transformation* — A *Select Annotated Bibliography of Special Programmes* (Hyderabad, NIRD, 1984).

Nilamani Senapati and Durga Charan Kumar, *Orissa. District Gazetter Boudh-Kandhamals* (Bhubaneshwar, Government of Orissa Publication).

Nirad C. Choudhry, *Hinduism* (New Delhi, B.I. Publications, 1979).

O. Peter and M. David, *Approaches to Participation in Rural Development* (Geneva, LLO, 1984).

P. Ramaiah, *Tribal Economy in India* (New Delhi, Light and Life Publishers, 1985).

P.C. Deb and B. K. Agrawal, *Rural Leadership in Green Revolution* (Delhi. CSIR : Research Publication, 1974).

P.R. Bose and V.N. Vashisth, *Rural Development and Technology—A Status Report cum Bibliography* (New Delhi, Council of Scientific and Industrial Research, 1980).

P.R. Dubashi, *Policy and Performance—Agricultural and Rural Development in Post-Independent. India* (New Delhi, Sage, 1986).

P.R. Dubashi, *Rural Development Administration in India* (Mumbai, Popular, 1970).

Paul Hartmen and Others, *Mass Media and Village Life: An Indian Study* (New Delhi, Sage, 1989).

Planning Commission and *PEO Evaluation Report on the Working of the Community Projects and National Extension Service Blocks* (Delhi, Manager of Publications, 1956).

Planning Commission, *PEO Evaluation of Integrated Tiibal Development Projects* (New Delhi, Government of India, 1987).

Pradipta Roy and B.R. Patil, *Edited Manual for Block Level Planning (Delhi,* MacMillan, 1977).

Prakash G. Reddy, *Politics of Tribal Exploitation* (Delhi, Mittal Publications, 1987).

Prem Shankar, *Indian Village Society in Transition* (New Delhi, Commonwealth, 1988)

R. Ferroni M. Kanbur, *Poverty Conscious Restructuring of Public Expenditure* (Washington, World Book, 1990).

R. Palme Dutt, *India Today* (Calcutta, Manisha, 1970).

R.C. Arora, *Integrated Rural Development* (New Delhi, S. Chand and Company, 1979).

R.H. Dholakia, *Regional Disparity in Economic Growth in India* (Mumbai, Himalaya Publishing House, 1985).

R.N Tripathy *et al., Tribal Development Programmes in Keonjhar, Orissa—An Evaluation* (Hyderabad, National Institute of Rural Development, 1979).

R.P. Mishra and K.V. Sundaram, *Multi-level Planning and Integrated Rural Development in India* (New Delhi, Heritage, 1990).

R.R.S. Mehta, *Rural Leadership and Panchayat* (Chandigarh, Bahari, 1978).

Raj Singh, *Rural Development and Social Legislation—A Dilemma,* (New Delhi, Ajanta, 1986).

Rajni Kothari, *Democratic Polity arid Social Change in India—Crises* and *Opportunities* (Mumbai, Allied, 1976).

Ramashray Roy and R.K. Srivastava, *Dialogues on Development* (New Delhi, Sage, 1986).

Ranjit Singh, *Communication Technology for Rural Development* (Delhi, B. R. Publication, 1993).

Robert Chambers, *Rural Development — Putting the Last First* (London, Longman, 1983)

Robert Chambers, *Rural Development — Putting the Last First* (Longman, Scientific and Technical, 1988).

S. Maheswari. *Rural Development, in India — A Public Policy Approach* (New Delhi, Sage, 1985).

S. Sundaram, *Anti-Poverty Rural Development in India* (New Delhi, D.K. Publishers, 1984).

S.C. Dube, *India's Changing Villages Human Factors in Community Development* (London, Routledge and Kegan Paul, 1985).

S.C. Dube, *Social and Psychological Implications of Development* (New Delhi, Sage, 1987).

S.C. Dube, *Tribal Heritage of India (New* Delhi, Vikas, 1977).

S.C. Dutt, *Wild Tribes* of India (New Delhi, Cosmo Publications, 1984).

S.C. Jain, *Rural Development: Institutions and Strategies* (Jaipur, Rawat Publications, 1985).

S.C. Verma, *Millions in Poverty Grip — India's Rural Works Programme* (New Delhi, Kunj, 1984).

S.K. Mishra and V.K. Puri, *Indian Economy* (New Delhi, Himalaya Publishing House, 1998).

S.L. Deshi, *Tribal Ethnicity, Class and Integration* (Jaipur, Rawat Publications, 1990).

S.M. Lipset, *Political Man* (New Delhi, Arnold-Heinemann India, 1973).

S.N. Eisenstadt, *Modernisation—Protest and Change* (New York, 1966).

S.N. Mishra and others, *Participation and Development* (Delhi, NBO, 1984).

S.N. Mishra, *New Horizons of Rural Development Administration* (Delhi, Mittal, 1989).

S.P. Shukla, *WTO and the Nation-State: Of Annexes and Annexation—The State of India's Economy* (Delhi, Public Interest Research Group, 1995).

S.R. Ramdev, *On Getting People to Participate—Seven Case Studies* (New Delhi, Central Institute of Research and Training in Public Cooperation, 1971).

S.S. Tehkamali, *Rural Development and Social Change in India* (Delhi, D.K. Publishers, 1983).

Sachidananda, *Culture Change in Tribal Bihar: Munda and Oraon* (Calcutta, Firma K.L. Mukhopadhyaya, 1964).

Sachidananda, *Social Dimension of Agricultural Development* (Delhi, National Publishing House, 1972).

Samuel P. Huntington, *Political Order in Changing Societies* (Princeton, Yale University Press, 1968).

Sartaz Aziz, *Rural Development, Learning from China* (London, MacMillan Press, 1978).

Satyendra Tripathy, *Development for the Rural Poor* (Jaipur, Rawat Publication, 1987).

Shiv R. Mehta, *Emerging Pattern of Rural Leadership* (New Delhi, Wiley Eastern, 1977).

Shiv R. Mehta, *Rural Development Policies and Programmes: — A Sociological Perspective* (New Delhi, Sage, 1984).

Sib Nath Bhattacharya, *Rural Development in India and Other Developing Countries* (New Delhi, Metropolitan Book, 1983).

Sukhomoy Chakravarthy, *Development Planning—The Indian Experience,* (New York, 1987).

Sydney Verba, *Participation and Political Equality: A Seven-Nation Comparison* (Cambridge, Cambridge University Press, 1978).

T. Vijayendra and Others, *Reservation of Jobs for Scheduled Castes and Tribes* (New Delhi, Human Futures, 1982).

T.H. Lewin, *Wild Races in the Eastern Frontier of India* (Delhi, Mittal Publishers, 1984).

T.K. Oomen, *Social Transformation in Rural India* (New Delhi, Vikas, 1984).

T.M. Dak, *Social Inequalities and Rural* Development (New Delhi, National, 1982).

T.N. Chaturvedi, *Rural Development—Some Themes and Dimensions* (New Delhi, Indian Institute of Public Administration, 1986).

T.R. Batten, *Non-Directive Approach in Group and Community Work* (London, Oxford, 1975).

Tribal Culture Research and Training Institute, *Evaluation Study Report on Tribal Development Programmes of ITDA Palmancha Khammam District* (Hyderabad, Tribal Welfare Department: Andhra Pradesh, 1986).

Tum Gabriel, *The Human Factor in Rural Development* (London, Beethoven Press, 1991).

U.K. Srivastava and P.S. George, *Rural Development in Action—The Experience of a Voluntary Agency* (Mumbai, Somaiya Publication, 1977).

UNDP. *Human Development. Report 1990* (New York, Oxford University Press, 1990).

UNDP, *Human Development Report 1993* (New York, Oxford University Press, 1993).

UNDP, *Human Development Report 1997* (New York, Oxford University Press, 1997).

United Nations, *Local Level Planning and Rural Development: Alternative Strategies* (New Delhi, Concept, 1980).

Vasant Desai, *Rural Development—6 Volumes* (Mumbai, 1988).

Vasudeva Rao, *Faces of Rural Development in India* (New Delhi, Asish, 1988).

W.E. Moore, *Industrialisation and Labour : Social Aspects of Economic Development* (New York, Cornell University Press, 1951).

William Kapp, *Hindu Culture, Economic Development and Economic Planning in India* (Illinois : New York, Patterson and Company, 1961).

William W. Biddle and Louride J. Biddle, *Community Development Process: The Rediscovery of Local Initiative* (New York, 1965).

DISSERTATIONS

A.K. Parida, *Technology and Rural Development in India: A Macro Sociological Analysis* (New Delhi, JNU M. Phil. Dissertation, 1986).

Arun Patnaik, *Power Structure and Rural Development Programme: A Study of Digapachandi Block in Orissa* (New Delhi, JNU M. Phil. Dissertation, 1984).

R.C. Mishra, *Bureaucracy and Rural Development — A Case Study of Mayurbhanj District of Orissa 1980–83, M. Phil. Dissertation* (New Delhi, J.N.U. M. Phil. Dissertation, 1983).

EDITED BOOKS

A.D. Moodie, ed., *Approaches to Rural Development* (Mumbai, Leslie Sawhny Programme of Training for Democracy, Friedrich-Naumann-Stiftung, 1976), pp. 1–7.

Ajit K. Danda, ed., *Studies on Rural Development —Experiences and Issues* (New Delhi, Inter-India, 1984).

Alfred Gell, "New Comers to the World of Goods Consumption Among the Maria Gonds", In Arjun Appadorai, ed., *The Social Life of Things: Commodities in Cultural Perspective* (Cambridge, Cambridge University Press, 1985).

Andre Beteille, "The Definition of a Tribe" in Romesh Thapar, ed., *Tribe, Caste and Religion in India* (Delhi, Mac- Millan India Ltd, 1977), pp. 7–14.

B.B. Chatterji, ed., *Micro Studies on Community Development, Panchayati Raj and Cooperation* (Delhi, Sterling, 1969).

Bharat Patankar and Gail Omvedt, "Perspective for the Administration and Development of Scheduled Tribes" in V.R.K. Paramahansa, ed., *Perspective on Tribal Development and Administration* (Hyderabad, National Institute of Community Development, 1975).

B.K. Roy Burman, "Perspectives for Administration and Development of Scheduled Tribes" in V.R.K. Paramahansa, ed., *Perspectives on Tribal Development and Administration* (Hyderabad, NICD, 1975).

B.M. Desai, ed., *Intervention for Rural Development — Experiences of the Small Formers' Development Agency* (Ahmedabad, Indian Institute of Management, 1977).

D.K. Maitra, "Experiences in Organising Economic Activities" in B.M. Desai ed., *Intervention for Rural Development* (Ahmedabad, IIM, 1977).

D.R. Shah, ed., *Alternatives in Rural Development* (New Delhi, Sterling, 1990).

D.W. Arwood and B.S. Baviskar, ed., *Who Shares? Cooperation and Rural Development* (Mumbai, Oxford University Press, 1988).

David, A.M. Lea and D.P. Choudhury, ed., *Rural Development and the State* (London, Metheun, 1983).

E. Evans-Pritchard and M. Fortes, ed., *African Political Systems* (London, International African Institute, 1940).

Elliot R. Morris and David D. Gow, ed., *Implementing Rural Development Projects — Lessons from Air and World Bank Experiences* (Boulder, West View Press, 1985).

F.L. Brayne, ed., *Better Villages* (Mumbai, Oxford University Press, 1945).

Gabriel Almond and James Coleman, ed., *The Politics of Developing Areas* (Princeton, Princeton University Press, 1960).

Gail Omvedt, ed., *Land, Caste and Politics in Indian States* (Delhi, Authors' Guild, 1982).

H. Glickman, "Political Science" in R.A. Lystad, ed., *The African World—A Survey of Social Research* (New York, Praeger, 1965).

I.S. Kingra, "Performance of SFDA and its programmes, Sirmur District, Himanchal Pradesh in B.M. Desai, ed., *Intervention for Rural Development—Experiences of the Small Farmers Development Agency* (Ahmedabad, Indian Institute of Management, 1977).

J.F. Johnes, "An Introduction to Social Development" in J.F. Jones and R.S. Pandey, ed., *Social Development: Conceptual, Methodological and Policy Issues* (New Delhi, Mac Millan, 1981).

J.R. Rele and M.K. Jain, ed., *Population, Change and Development in India* (Deonar, International Institute for Population Studies, 1978).

J. Owen Jones, Economic and Social Aspects of Rural Development", in Ajit K. Danda, ed., *Studies in Rural Development — Experiences and Issues* (New Delhi, Inter India, 1984).

Jagannath Pathy, "An Outline of Mode of Production in Tribal India" in Buddhadev Choudhury, ed., *Tribal Development in India: Problems and Prospects* (New Delhi, Inter-India, 1982).

Joseph La Plambora and Myron Weiher, ed., *Political Parties and Political Development* (Princeton, Princeton University Press, 1966).

Julio Boltvinik, "Poverty Measurement and Alternative Indicators of Development", In Rolph Van Der Hoeven and Richard Anker, ed., *Poverty Monitoring — An International Concern* (Mew York, St. Martin Press, 1991), pp. 84–94.

K. Amnachalam and K.M. Natarajan, ed., *Integrated Rural Development* (Madurai, Koolal Publication, 1977).

K.L. Sharma, ed., *Social Stratification in India* (New Delhi, Manohar Publications, 1986), pp. 79–87.

K.S. Singh. ed., *Economics of the Tribes and Their Transformations (New* Delhi, Concept Publishing Co. 1982).

K.S. Singh 'Tribal Land Organisation in Chhotanagpur and its Development". In *Trends of Socio-Economic Change in India* (Simla, Indian Institute of Advance Study, 1969).

K.S. Singh, "From Ethnicity to Regionalism: A Study in Tribal Politics and Movements in Chhotanagpur from 1900 to 1975 in S.C. Malik, ed., *Dissent, Protest and Reform in Indian Civilisation* (Simla, Indian Institute of Advanced Study, 1977).

Kirti S. Parikh, ed., *India Development Report—1997* (Delhi, Oxford University Press, 1997).

Kurukshetra, ed., *A Symposium on Rural Development* (New Delhi, Publication Division, 1961).

L. P. Vidyarthi and B.K. Rai, *The Tribal Culture of India* (Delhi, Concept, 1977).

L.P. Vidyarthi, ed., *Rural Development in south Asia* (New Delhi, Concept, 1982).

Laliti K. Sen, ed., *Readings on Micro-level Planning and Rural Growth Centres* (Hyderabad, National Institute of Community Development, 1972).

Lucien Pye, "Democracy, Modernisation and Nation-Building" in J.R. Pennock, ed., *Self-Government in Modernising Nations* (Engelwood Cliffs: New Jeresy, Prentice- Hall, 1964), pp. 6–25.

M.A.K. Beg and others, ed., *Basic Needs and Rural Development* (Karachi, Pakistan Academy of Rural Development, 1980).

M.J. Campbell, ed., *New Technology and The Rural Impact* (London, Routledge, 1990).

McKim Mariot and Ronald Inden, "Towards an Ethno-Sociology of South Asian Caste Systems" in David Kenneth, ed., *The New Wind* (The Hague, Mouten, 1977)

P.D. Malgavkar, "Marketing Approaches of the Village and Small Industries to Rural Development" in A.D. Moodie, ed., *Approaches to Rural Development* (New Delhi, Inter India, 1984).

P.K. Bhowmik, "Approaches to Tribal Welfare" in Buddhadev Choudhury, ed., *Tribal Development in India: Problems and Prospects* (Delhi, Inter-India, 1982).

P.R. Brahmanand and Others, ed., *Dimension of Rural Development in India* (Mumbai, Himalaya Publishing House, 1987).

Paul Cloke, ed., *Politics and Plans for The Rural People — An International Perspective* (London, Unwin Hyman, 1988).

Peter Von Blackenburg, "Organisational Aspects of Mobilisation of People in Integrated Rural Development" in Ajit K. Danda, ed., *Studies on Rural Development—Experiences and Issues* (New Delhi, Inter India, 1984).

Phjilip Viegas and Geeta Menon, "Development Pattern, Forest Policy and Exploitation of Tribals" in Walter Fernadez, ed., *Inequality, its Bases and Search for Solutions: Dr. Alfred D'Souza Memorial Essays* (New Delhi, India Social Institute, 1986), pp. 57–84.

R.P. Mishra and K.V.S. Sundaran, ed., *Rural Area Development — Perspective and Approaches* (New Delhi, Sterling, 1979).

R.P. Mishra, "Growth Centres and the Rural Urban Continuum" in A.D. Moodie, ed., *Approaches to Rural Development* (Mumbai, Leslie Sawhny Programme of Training for Democracy, Friedrich-Naumann—Stiftung, 1976), pp. 49–65.

R. Srinivasan, "Lending to the Farmer", In A.D. Moodie, ed., *Approaches to Rural Development* (Mumbai, Leslie Sawhny Programme of Training for Democracy, Friedrich-Naumann— Stiftung, 1976), pp. 29–41.

R. Subramaniam, ed., *Rural Development—An Inside Look at Problems and Prospects* (New Delhi, Yatan Publication, 1988).

Rabi Kunbur, "Poverty and Development: The Human Development Report (1990) and the World Development Report (1990) in Rolph Van Der Hoeven and Richard Anker, ed., *Poverty Monitoring* — An *International Concern* (New York, St. Martin Press), pp. 81–94.

Ranan Weitz, ed., *Rural Development in a Changing World* (Cambridge, MIT, 1971).

Ranjit Gupta, ed., *Planning for Tribe Development* (New Delhi, Ankur Publishing House, 1976).

Raymond Apthrope, ed., *People, Planning and Development Studies Some Reflections on Social Planning* (London, Cass, 1970).

Rolph Van Der Hoeven and Rihard Anker, ed., *Poverty Monitoring : An International Concern* (Washington, St. Martin Press, 1990).

S. Alvi, ed., *Bureaucracy and Rural Development* (Karachi, Pakistan Academy of Rural Development, 1968).

S. Hansda, "Agricultural Development in Tribal Aeas", in S.N. Mishra and B. Singh ed., *Tribal Area Development* (New Delhi, Society for the Study of Regional Disparities, 1983), pp. 21–26.

S.N. Dubey and Ratna Mordia, ed., *Land Alienation and Restoration in* Sheo Kumar Lal and Umed Raj Nahar, ed., *Rural Social Transformation* (Jaipur, Rawat Publication, 1992).

T. Mathew, ed., *Rural Development in India-Seminar Papers on Rural Development read at the NEHU, April 1978* (New Delhi, Agricole, 1984).

T. K. Laxman and B. K. Narayan, ed., *Rural Development in India—A Multi Dimentional Analysis* (Mumbai, Himalaya Publishing House, 1984).

Thomas M. Fraser Jr, "Socio-Cultural Parameters in Directed Change", in Hari Mohan Mathur, ed., *Anthropology in the Development Process* (New Delhi, Vikas Publishing House, 1977).

Tribal Communities in India (Mumbai, Himalaya Publishing House, 1977).

V. K. Srivastava, ed., *Commercial Activities and Rural Development in South Asia—A Geographical Study* (New Delhi, Concept, 1988).

Walter Fernandez and R. Tandan, ed., *Participatory Research and Education* (New Delhi, Indian Social Institute, 1981).

Walter Fernandez, ed., *People's Participation in Development—Approaches to Non-Formal Education* (New Delhi, Indian Social Institute, 1980).

ARTICLES

A.K. Singh and Others, "The Myth of the Healthy Tribal", *Social Change* (New Delhi) January 1987, pp. 3–23.

A.K. Upadhyaya, "Peasantisation of Adivasis in Thane District" *Economic and Political weekly* (Mumbai), Vol. XXX No. 52, 1980, pp. A134–A146.

Ajit K. Danda, "Predicaments of a Forest Dwelling Tribe" *Journal of the Indian Anthropological Society*, (New Delhi) November 1990, pp. 215–22.

Amar Kumar Singh, "Development in Post Independence India: Quo Vadis? *"Social Change"* (New Delhi), 20(4), pp. 20–29.

Ashok Rudra, "One Step Forward, Two steps Backward", *Economic and Political Weekly* (Mumbai), Vol. XVI, No. 25–26, 1981.

B.B. Mandal, "Are Tribal Cultivators in Bihar to be Called Peasants?" *Man in India* (New Delhi) April, 1975.

B.N. Mohapatra and D. Bhattacharya, "Tribal-Dalit Conflict—Electoral Politics in Phulbani", *Economic and Political Weekly* (Mumbai), January 13–20, 1996, pp. 160–164.

B. Ramakrishna Reddy, "Language and Ethnic Identity: A case study of the Kandh Tribals", *Asian Studies,* April 1986, pp. 28–35.

Baren Ray, "Tribal Problem in India", *Mainstream* (New Delhi), January 20, 1990, pp. 28–30.

Bhupinder Singh, "Poverty Among Scheduled Tribes", *ASSI Quarterly* (New Delhi), January–June 1992, pp. 256–267.

Bikram Narayan Nanda, "Vernacular Work, Wage Labour and Tribal Development: A Case Study of Highland Orissa", *Contributions to India Sociology* (New Delhi), January–June 1992, pp. 115–132.

Burkhand Schnepel, "Corporations, Personhood and Ritual in Tribal Society: Three Interconnected Topics in the Anthropology of Meyer Forests" *Journal of the Anthropological Society of Oxford* (London), January 1990, pp. 1–31.

C. Subramanain, "A Strategy for Rural Development" in Ajit K. Danda, ed., *Studies on Rural Development : Experiences and Issues* (New Delhi, Inter-India, 1984).

Christopher Von Furer, Haimendorf, "Tribal Problem of India" *A Discourse at The National Institute of Rural Development* (Hyderabad), Dec. 18–27, 1985.

D.N. Dhanagare, "Subaltern Consciousness and Populism— Two Approaches in the Study of Social Movements in India" *Social Scientist,* November 1988, 11. 18–33.

David Baker, "State Policy, the Market Economy and Tribal Decline: The Central Provinces, 1861–1920", *Indian Economic and Social History Review,* Oct–Dec. 1991, pp. 341–370.

Dietmar Rothermund, "500 years of Colonialism", *Social Action* (New Delhi), January–March 1992, pp. 1–15.

Dolly Arora, "From State Regulation to People's Participation — Case of Forest Management in India", *Economic and Political Weekly* (Mumbai), March 19, 1994, pp. 691–697.

E. Keruppaiyan "Issues in Poverty Alleviation Programmes for the Tribals", *Social Action* (New Delhi), Jan–March 1989, pp. 72–82.

E.P.W. Da Costa, "Stimulation of Demand Through Agricultural Development" in A.D. Moodie, ed., *Approaches to Rural Development* (Mumbai, Leslie Sawhny Programme of Training for Democracy, Friedrich-Naumann-Stiftung, 1976).

Edgar Litt, "Political Cynicism and Political Futility", *Journal of Politics,* vol. 25, 1963, pp. 312–323.

F.G. Bailey, "Tribe and Caste in India" *Contributions to Indian Sociology* (New Delhi), No. 5, 1961, pp. 7–19.

Frank Lindenfield, "Economic Interest and Political Involvement", *Public Opinion Quarterly, 28,* 1964, pp. 104–111.

G.K. Lieten, "Caste, Gender and Class in Panchayats — Case of Bardhaman, West Bengal", *Economic and Political Weekly* (Mumbai) July 18, 1992, pp. 1567–1572.

Gail Omvedt, "Anti-Caste Movement and the Discourse of Power", *Race and Class* (London), Oct–Dec. 1991, pp. 15–28.

Gautam Kumar Bera, "Cultural Cost of Maria Ethnocide", *Journal of the Indian Anthropological Society* (New Delhi), July 1990, pp. 101–105.

Ghanashyam Shah, "Tribal Identity and Class Differentiation", *Economic and Political Weekly* (Mumbai), No. 4, 1979, pp. 459–64.

Ghulam Ghouse, "Financing the Farmers" in A.D. Moodie, ed., *Approaches to Rural Development,* (Mumbai, Leslie Sawhny Programme of Training for Democracy, Friedrich-Naumann-Stiftung, 1976).

H. McClosky, "Political Participation" in *International Encyclopaedia of Social Sciences* (New York, Collier-MacMillan, 1968) Vol. 12, p. 253.

H. Pais and C.S.K. Singh, "Rural Development Policies and Inequalities", *Social Action* (New Delhi), January–March 1987, pp. 28–44.

Harish C. Srivastava, "Socio-Economic and Demographic Profile of the Karar Tribe of Madhya Pradesh", *Man in India* (New Delhi), June 1990, pp. 101–122.

Harshad R. Trivedi, "Planning and Tribal Development", *Indian Journal of Public Administration* (New Delhi), April–June 1991, pp. 182–198.

Himansu Roy, "Tribal Society in Transition — A Case Study of Lohit District of Arunachal Pradesh", *Teaching Politics* (New Delhi), Vol. 16, 1990.

Hoshiar Singh, "Constitutional Base for Panchayati Raj in India", *Asian Survey* (Berkeley), September 1994, pp. 818–827.

I.C. Awasthi, "Decentralisation Perspectives and Rural Development", *Social Charge* (New Delhi), September 1991, pp. 47–50.

J.J. Roy Burman, "Shifting Cultivation—As Aspect of Tribal Exploitation", *Indian Journal of Social Work* (New Delhi), January 1990, pp. 57–73.

Jagannath Pathy, "Idea of Tribe and the Indian Scene", *Man in India* (New Delhi), December 1989, pp. 346–58.

Jagannath Pathy, "Political Economy of Kandhaland", *Man in India* (New Delhi), 56(1), pp. 1–36.

Jagannath Pathy, Suguna Paul, Manu Bhaskar and Jayaram Panda, *"Tribal Studies in India : An Appraisal", Eastern Anthropologist* (Calcutta), 29(4), 1976, pp. 399–417.

Jawaharlal Nehru, "Pandit Nehru's Views About the Scheduled Tribes", *Tribal Research Bulletin,* March 1989 (Nehru's Speech Given in 1952).

K. John Mammen, "Perceptions of Poverty", *Indian Express* (New Delhi) March 4, 1988.

K.C. Alexander, "Dimensions and Indications of Development", Journal of Rural Development (Hyderabad), Vol. 12(3) 1993, pp. 257-267.

K.P. Kumaran, "Cultural Dimensions of Development" *Social Change* (New Delhi), December 1991, pp. 15–21.

K.R.G. Nair, "New Economic Policy and Development of Backward Regions: A Note on Orissa", *Economic and Political Weekly* (Mumbai), May 8, 1993.

K.S. Singh, "Environment, Technology and Management in Rural Areas", *Man in India* (New Delhi) January 1990, pp. 123–130.

K.S. Singh, "Hinduism and Tribal Religion—An Anthropological Perspective", *Man in India* (New Delhi), March 1993, pp. 1–16.

K.S. Singh, "State Formation in Tribal Societies—Some Preliminary Observations", *Journal of Indian Anthropology* (Calcutta), VI, 1971, pp. 161–81.

K.S. Singh, "Transformation of Tribal Society: Integration *Versus* Assimilation", *Economic and, Political Weekly,* (Mumbai), 17(33) : 1982, pp. 1376–1384.

K.S. Singh, "Tribal Violence", *Journal of the Anthropological Survey of India* (Calcutta) June–September 1990, pp. 127–132.

K. Sundaram and Suresh V. Tendulkar, "Integrated Rural Development Programme in India", *Social Action* (New Delhi) Vol. 35, January–March 1985, pp. 1–25.

Kailash Sarap, "Collateral and Other Forms of Guarantee in Rural Credit Markets : Evidence from Eastern India", *Indian Economic Review,* July–Dec. 1991, pp. 167–188.

Kailash Sarap, "Factors Anecting Small Farmers Access to Institutional Credit in Rural Orissa, India", *Development and. Change* (New Delhi Sage, April 1990), pp. 281–308.

Kancha Illaiah, "SCs and STs Systemic Exploitation" *Economic and Political Weekly* (Mumbai), December 1990, pp. 2771–2774.

L. Bharara, "Indian Pastoral Community Following Live Stock Migration as a Drought Adjustment Strategy", *Journal of the Anthropological Survey of India* (Calcutta), 42(1), March 1993, pp. 30–54.

Leela Dushkin, "Backward Class, Benefits and Social Class in India", *Economic and Political Weekly* (Mumbai), 7 April 1979.

Leo Strole, "Social Integration and Certain Corollaries — An Explanatory Study", *American Sociological Review,* 21, 1956, pp. 709–716.

M. Jagadeswar Rao and M.B. Shankar Rao, "Tribal Development in India — Some Facets", Nirnaya, September 1989, pp. 1–10.

M. Jayaraju, "IRDP in Eliminating Poverty Among the Scheduled Castes and Scheduled Tribes", *Economic Affairs,* 38(2), April–June 1993, pp. 111–113.

M. Sahay and A.K. Singh, "Modernity in Tribal Hindus" *Social Change* (New Delhi), 19(4), 1989, pp. 74–92.

M.D. Mistry, "People's Research and Mobilisation : Drought Relief and Minimum Wages, *Social Action* (New Delhi), January–March 1989, pp. 58–71.

M.L. Santhanam and D. Namasivayam "Correlates of People's Participation" *Social Change* (New Delhi) Vol. 20, No. 1, March 1990.

M.L. Santhanam, C. Yoganand Sastry, S. Vijaya Kumar, "People's Participation; Some Psychological Dimensions", *Journal of Rural Development* (Hyderabad), 3(4), pp. 249–329.

M.Z. Khan and M.E. Thomas "Administrative Support to Socio-Economic Programmes for the Tribals", *Social Action* (New Delhi), January–March 1989, pp. 3–15.

Madras Institute of Development Studies "Structure and Intervention — An Evaluation of DAAP, IRDP and Related Programmes in Ramanathpuram and Dharampuri District of Tamil Nadu", (Madras, MIDS, 1980).

Mohan K. Singhania, 'Tribes and National Integration in India", *Man in India* (New Delhi), December 1991, pp. 269–338.

Moris Rosenberg, "Some Determinants of Political Apathy, *Public Opinion Quarterly,* 18, 1954, pp. 34–66.

N.V.N, Rao and P. Raman Reddy, "Minor Irrigation and Tribal Development : An Empirical Study" Kurukshetra, Vol. 34, No. 2, 1985, pp. 31–33.

Nafisa Suga D'Souza, "Landholding Systems in the Tribal Area", *Social Action* (New Delhi) July–September 1991, pp. 345–350.

National Institute of Health and Family Welfare, "An Evaluation of Community Health Workers," *NIHFW Reports* (New Delhi) 1978 & 1979.

Nila Umesh, "Enterpreneurship Among Tribals — A New Approach" *Link* (New Delhi), 12 September 1993, pp. 16–21.

Nirmal Mukherji, 'The Third Stratum" *Economic and Political Weekly*, May 1, 1993, pp. 859–862

Nirmal Sengupta "Social and Economic Basis of Current Tribal Movements", *Social Action* (New Delhi) 40(4), October–December 1990, pp. 336–346.

Nirmal Sengupta, Reappraising Tribal Movements : Legitimation and Spread — I, II, III, IV, *Economic and Political Weekly*, May 7–28, 1988, pp. 951–943, pp. 1003–1005, pp. 1054–1056, p. 1112.

Nita Mathur, "Evolving Strategies for Tribal Development", Strategies for Tribal Development", *Mainstream* (New Delhi) 7 March 1992, pp. 17–22.

P. Acharya, "Panchayats and Left-Politics in West Bengal" *Economic and Political Weekly* (Mumbai), May 29, 1993, pp. 1080–1082.

P. Panda and others, "Integrated Child Development Scheme: A Case Study" *Indian Journal of Social Work* (New Delhi) October 1990, pp. 583–594.

P. Ramaiah and others, "Impact of Technology on Tribal Agriculture: A Micro study" *Khadi Gramodyoga* , November 1990, pp. 77–84.

P.K. Bhowmick, "Concept of Diseases and Disease Gods and Goddesses", *Journal of Social Research* (Calcutta), Vol. 2, No. 2, pp. 7–22.

P.K. Bhowmick, 'Tribes in the Changing Circumstances of India", Man *in India* (New Delhi), March 1991, Special Issue, pp. 151–162.

P.S.K. Menon and D.K. Roy, "Land Alienation in Tribal Areas", A Paper Presented at the *NIRD Course on Tribal Culture and Development* (Hyderabad), December 18–27, 1985.

Partho Dasgupta, "Well-being and the Extent of its Realisation in Poor Countries", *The Economic Journal* (London), Conference Issue 1990, pp. 1–32.

Prabhat Patnaik and C.P. Chandrasekhar, "Indian Economy under Structural Adjustment", *Economic and Political Weekly* (Mumbai), November 25, 1995.

Pradhan H. Prasad, "Panchayati Raj and People's Movement", *Mainstream,* New Delhi, March 4, 1995, pp. 6–7.

Pramod Kumar Rai, "Study of Authoritarianism Rigidity and Dogmatism in Tribal and Non-Tribal Youth" *Indian Psychological Review,* August–October 1989, pp. 1–7.

Pranab K. Dasgupta, "Industrilisation and Tribal Development" *Journal of Anthropological Survey of India* (Calcutta) June–September 1990, pp. 143–50.

Programme Evaluation Organisations, "Evaluation Report (1980a) of Food for Work Programme—August–October 1979, (New Delhi) 1980.

Programme Evaluation Organisations, "Report (1979a) on the Evaluation Study of Small Farmers Marginal Farmers and Agricultural Labourers Projects" (New Delhi), 1979.

Programme Evaluation Organisations, "Report (1979c) of Study for Crash Scheme for Rural Employment—1971-74, 1979.

R.H.Kanbur, " Measurement and Alleviation of Poverty", *I MF Staff Papers,* (Washington), 1987.

R.K. Jain, "Seasonal Migration of Tribal Labour", *Economic and Political Weekly* (Mumbai), Vol. XIV, 1979, pp. 1727–1732.

R.K. Samanta, "The Political Economy of Panchayati Raj in West Bengal" *Social Change* (New Delhi) March 1990.

R.N. Tripathy *et al.*, 'Tribal Development Programmes in Keonjhar, Orissa—An Evaluation" *NIRD* (Hyderabad), 1979.

R.V. Bhuskute, "Tribals, Dalits and Government Lands", *Economic and Political Weekly* (Mumbai), October 21, 1989, pp. 2355–2358.

Rajesh Kumar, "Can Panchayati Raj Succeed Without Land Reforms?" Manstream (New Delhi) March 4, 1995, p. 8.

Ralph C. Meyer and David S. Malcolm, "Voting in India: Effects on Economic Change and New Party Formation", *Asian Survey* (Berkeley), May 1993, pp. 507–519.

Ramesh Chandekar and Gracious Thomas, "Factors Influencing People's Participation", *Social Change* (New Delhi), March 1990.

Reserve Bank of India, "The Small Farmers Development Agencies—A Field Study" *RBI Report* (Mumbai) 1975.

Roger Paint, "International Community and Land Rights for Indigenous and Tribal Peoples" *Development.* (London) No. 4, 1992. pp. 18–93.

S. Basaliah and Govind S. Gouda, "Socio-Economic Profiles of Family Planning : Adopters and Non-Adopters" *Social Change* (New Delhi) Vol. 2, Nos. 3 and 4, pp. 45–48

S. Mahalingam and V. Rajendran, "Marketing of Agricultural Produces through Tribal Cooperatives—Replica of Twang Model in North East India" *Journal of Rural Development* (Hyderabad), March 1991, pp. 159–170.

S. Mahalingam, Economic Regeneration of Landless Tribals in Mizoram," *Social Change* (New Delhi), June 1991, pp. 54–58.

S.C. Ghosal, "Effects of Jhum Cultivation on a Tribal Community," *Human Science,* December 1989, pp. 2956–99.

S.K. Choudhury , "Tribal Development : Dimensions of Planning and Implementation", *Indian Anthropologist* (New Delhi) June–December 1990, pp. 49–66.

S.P. Punalekar, "Land Mobility and Social Status—A Case of Tribal Community", *New Quest* (Mumbai) January–February 1996, pp. 39–44.

Sharad Patil, "Mobilising Scheduled Castes and Scheduled Tribes" *Economic and Political Weekly* (Mumbai), September 1989, pp. 2002–2006.

Sophia Khanum Pathen, "Religious Beliefs and Practices of the People in Karnataka Village" *Journal of Social Research* Vol. 2, No. 2, pp. 65–73.

Stuart Carbridge, "Tribal Politics, Finance and the State: The Jharkhand India 1900–1980", *Ethnic and Racial Studies* (London), April 1989, pp. 175–208.

Subhadra Chanana and B.K. Srivastava, "Tribal Welfare: Problems and Prospects" *Mainstream* (New Delhi) May 1990, pp. 15–16 and 22.

Surajit Sinha, "Tribal Cultures of Peninsular India as a Dimension of Little Tradition in the Study of Indian Civilization: A Preliminary Statement" *Journal of American Folklore* (New York), 1958, pp. 504–518.

Surjit Sinha, "Tribe-Caste and Tribe-Peasent Continua in Central India", *Man in India* (New Delhi) 45, 1, 1965.

T. Madhara Menon, "Tribal Identity : A Language and Communication Perspective—A Review Article". *International Journal of Dravidian Linguistics,* June 1992, pp. 126–129.

T.K. Moulik and Others, "Bio-Gas System in India—A Socio-Economic Evaluation, *Paper Published Under Auspices of Indian Institute of Management* (Ahmedabad) 1978.

U. Lele, "Cooperatives and the Poor: A Comparative Perspective", A *World Development* 9(1) 1981, pp. 55–72.

V.M. Dandekar and N. Rath, "Poverty in India", *Economic and Political Weekly* (Mumbai) 1971.

Vidya Das, "Conservation, Government and Tribal People" *Economic and Political Weekly* (Mumbai), March 21, 1992.

Walter Fernandez and Arundhati Roy Choudhury, "Search for a Tribal Identity: The Dominant and the Sub-Altern", *Social Action* (New Delhi), January-March 1993, pp. 8–21.

Walter Fernandez, "Forest Policy : A Solution to Tribal Deprivation?" *Indian Journal of Social Work* (New Delhi), January 1990, pp. 35–56.

Walter Fernandez, "Power and Powerlessness—Development Projects and Displacement of Tribals" *Social Action* (New Delhi) July–September 1991, pp. 243–270.

William G. Vanderbok, "The Mobilisation and Alignment of the Indian Electorate", *British Journal of Political Science* (London), April 1990, pp. 237–262.

William Erbe, "Social Involvement and Political Activity", *American Sociological Review* (29), 1964, pp. 198–215.

INDEX

❑❑❑